CAPITOL HELLWAY MEDIA COMPANY

Petition to the Government for a Redress of Grievances

"The Edwards Dossier"

a free media company in
NAPLES FLORIDA

First published by Capitol Hellway Media Company LLC 2020

Library of Congress Control Number: 2020914851

First edition

ISBN: 978-1-7355363-3-0

Illustration by Cathy Edwards

This book was professionally typeset on Reedsy.
Find out more at reedsy.com

for all
Human Beings

~ ~ ~

and especially my gorgeous wife, Cathy

"Masks. Vaccines. Abortions.
Before you know it,
our women will be made to wear hoods."

John Stuart Edwards
an American writer
early 21st century

Contents

III What are your frustrations? Here are some of mine.

#545Rule300

On Labor Day 2020, 545 people in the United States government ruled more than 300 million people. The country was being ripped apart.

The U.S. was waging an internal war with domestic Marxist affiliated revolutionaries and a rogue coronavirus. Tensions between the United States and China were escalating and tyranny was threatening the entire world. Knowledge was replaced with passionate cries for social justice from the mob.

The writings of **John Stuart Edwards** are intended to scratch the consciousness of humans to lean toward freedom. His full archive can be accessed with the keyword #545Rule300 on any platform or database in the world, *one day*. It is his gift for all humans & the **key** to all Knowledge for all time.
#545Rule300

Petition to the Government for a Redress of Grievances

a.k.a. "The Edwards Dossier"
confirmed delivery on October 7, 2019 to

U.S. Congressman Mario Diaz-Balart
Florida-25th District
8669 N.W. 36 Street, #100
Doral, FL 33166
(305) 470-8555

Dear Legislative, Executive & Judicial Branches of the United States Government:

The **Capitol Hellway Media Company LLC** presents our official *Petition to the Government for a Redress of Grievances* featuring contributions by American writer **John Stuart Edwards** and American artist **Cathy Edwards**. Capitol Hellway is a free media company in Naples, Florida.

"Words have precise meaning only to the person who wrote them. The construct of knowledge gained from words over time is a creative endeavor. Words are the shape of an equation. Some people play chess, some play checkers, and some play something else or nothing at all to gain knowledge. Knowledge is experimentation and tests. Knowledge is trial and error. Knowledge is passing and failing and failing again, but always getting up. Knowledge is gained with words always in motion and free. Knowledge is in the mind. Knowledge is honesty and trust. **Do Not Restrict Free Speech**. Ignorance is when freedom is lost. Knowledge is everything we have been and become."

The Edwards Knowledge Equation with **#545Rule300** is John Stuart Edwards' contribution to help freedom loving people eliminate all corruption across the entire federal government immediately using the tools provided to us by the Founders, and secure the future of the **American Dream** for all **humans** for all time by solving important problems in the world.

confirmed delivery on October 7, 2019 to
U.S. Congressman Mario Diaz-Balart

Course Syllabus

Petition to the Government for a Redress of Grievances

> *"It is forbidden to kill; therefore all murderers are punished unless they kill in large numbers and to the sound of trumpets."*
> *Voltaire*

The purpose of this course is to introduce readers to freedom of thought and expression in the public square.

RESEARCH TOPICS

The Future of Human Life

- *During the next half-century, disease prevention and cellular regeneration can transform health care and extend life.*
- *Community ecosystems in the United States can become environmentally secure.*
- *Wire-free transmission networks and receivers can provide ubiquitous electricity and communications anywhere around the globe.*
- *Nourishment technologies can transform molecules into potable water and revolutionize the production and portability of food and medicine.*
- *Problem solving can be unconstrained by biological intelligence that is supplemented with AI.*

- *Robotics can transform transportation, services and manufacturing economies.*
- *And the world can have peace.*

Class Culture

- React Research Respond

The Edwards Knowledge Equation

- *$K=(q-a)/t$*
- *The Two Functions of Time /t*

What are your Grievances? Here are some of mine.

- *Case Studies on Federal Government Corruption, Malfeasance and Reform*

Research Expeditions

"What the hell do you have to lose?"

John Stuart Edwards
the creator of this course
johnstuartedwards.com

Leader Guide

React Research Respond

For each chapter, students will read and **react** to the chapter at first reading, conduct some **research** and then **respond**.

PART ONE

Class Culture

3 R's Practice Session 1

PART TWO

The Edwards Knowledge Equation

PART THREE

Case Studies on Federal Government Corruption, Malfeasance and Reform

3 R's Practice Session 2

PART FOUR

Research Expeditions in the Real World

The Future of Human Life

I

Class Culture

Practice Session 1

Oxymoron's are US

Insurrection is the Rule of Law
The Future of Human Life

React Research Respond

The 3 R's

The purpose of this textbook is to introduce readers to freedom of thought and expression in the public square in order to facilitate solutions to humanity's biggest problems.

For students, participation is required in person or by electronic means. There is no limitation to class size. This textbook is for mature audiences.

`React Research Respond`

For each chapter, readers will read and **react** to the chapter at first reading, conduct some **research** and then **respond** in a class setting.

o·ver·re·act

`what humans do when they skip over the research step.`

This is the First edition.

Case study substitution is encouraged. The **React Research Respond** method described in this textbook is applicable to all human learning and free for anyone to use in any manner they choose for all time.

Capitol Hellway Media Company LLC

Editorial published on July 4, 2020

Democrats Are Not Smart Or Evil

What if some earlier generation wiped away some history before it was discovered? Imagine all the knowledge that would have been lost. Imagine a world without the Dead Sea Scrolls, Nazca Lines, The Library of Ashurbanipal, The Rosetta Stone, Terracotta Army, Moai, Pompeii, Tomb of Tutankhamun, Machu Picchu and Troy.

For the reason I explain below, today, I call for everyone employed in **academia** who supported the mob destruction of any monument to be publicly humiliated, perp walked if possible, and fired. These demons have cast evil upon our children's lives!

For all the "academics" that said they want for our police, I want a national database to ensure you can never work anywhere across the country in academia; I want all your union "immunity" benefits stripped from your rights, and I want Congress to pass that bill tomorrow so we can put an end to your career before the fall semester starts.

Academics that called for the removal of any history by force are unfit to teach our youth. They are committing academic malpractice and must be sued for the damages they have done and be fired!

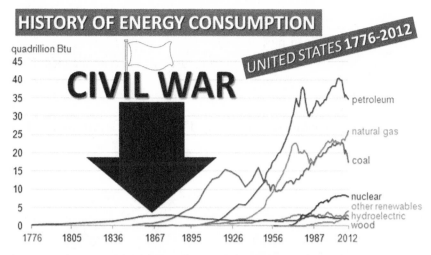

Source: *United States Energy Information Administration*

"How many of you have ever heard of DOS disks? If you were born after 1975, unless your dad was a geek, you may not remember that DOS is an acronym for disk operating system. In the late 20th Century, humans led by Bill Gates and Steve Jobs built the largest commercial industry in the entire history of the world - digital machinery. It began with an appliance and media that could store instructions. Some of you remember the IBM 360 when punching 80 column cards was how you wrote programs. Collections of 1's and O's organized with spaces and sequenced on tape. Prior to the 20th Century during the Civil War, fuel and machinery worked together. Petroleum was just beginning to be discovered. Humans in the late 19th Century discovered new forms of energy in the world beginning at the start of the U.S. Civil War. Humans in the late 20th Century invented the computer industry in order to control all energy use and thereby, control all knowledge. In the year 2020, the Democrats won...."

And this story, written in the future by an 18 year old, goes on from there to support its thesis by describing what happened in history... but wait! It doesn't. This story was never written. It was never thought. It was never whispered. It was never part of the **K**nowledge of the time.

Because the Civil War was erased from history. It never happened. It was gone.

Democrats are not smart or evil. They are not smart *and* evil.

~

Free Advertisement

DO YOU SUPPORT Marxism?

Since history can be erased, this textbook begins with a warm up assignment for readers to practice freedom of thought and expression in the public square. It is intended to be a safe place to practice the **React Research Respond** method described in chapter one before embarking on your research expedition.

Founding Father John Adams said, "Liberty, once lost, is lost forever," and Thomas Jefferson said, "All tyranny needs to gain a foothold is for people of good conscience to remain silent." Here is what they meant.

The little wind-up toys we see masquerading as humans in our cities this summer have all been programmed to think one way. Like computer software. The reason many Americans have a hard time organizing to stop this mass hysteria is because we elect politicians to protect us from criminals. And when the politicians don't do their jobs, the system breaks down and revolutionaries can attack. We are under attack. Black Lives Matter is the public relations department for a Marxist revolutionary militia with a mission to destroy American civilization and rebuild it into a utopia run by oligarchs. You will not hear that on the propaganda news outlets run by corrupt corporate media elites. Media corporations are controlled by billionaires who fund Black Lives Matter. Hence, widespread corporate buy-in to the Marxist ideology – till the next shareholder meeting. And that is where the billionaires will pick up the slack, or the U.S. Treasury will print more dollars until it all collapses, which is the whole point.

Command, control & communications – the 3 C's of an insurgency. Now we can openly say "corporations, media & communicating" the Black

Lives Matter brand. The battlespace is defined, but like every successful insurgency the enemy is difficult, but not impossible to identify.

And of course there are the militia operating on the ground, with medics and pre-positioned stockpiles of weapons for destruction in the cities they torment. These small trained units carry out tactical assaults to sow division by triggering strong emotions in vulnerable people through a carefully orchestrated blend of propaganda & truth. Terrorists hide in population centers. Rioters hide in protests. They tap the 'feelings' center of the brain so logic is no cure. It's like an infection, a mental disease. It is brainwashing at the highest form. These people are experts at leveraging the First Amendment to pry open the doors for their insurgency to pass through. Isolate and then silence the enemy. "COVID anyone? Don't protest unless it is for something we say is righteous. Then it is ok," the media tells us. It is exactly the playbook that our CIA has used to topple many other countries since WWII. It's happening here, today, in the United States of America. Black Lives Matter is just a brand. It is a brainwashing instrument for the media and academia to indoctrinate the most vulnerable people in our society – the guilty oppressors and the oppressed. The vast majority of people don't participate in this madness. They are you.

The Black Lives Matter brand is very popular and appealing to its worshipers and circumstantial guests. Its militias are well trained and organized and funded and agile. They go by many names. But what else besides the media billionaires are behind the malcontents wearing the 'Black Lives Matter' disguise? We now know the co-founders are "trained organizers," and "trained Marxists." So what do these Marxists want? What is the purpose of their revolution? Could their goal be to educate civilization on how to be civilized?

How Marxism is taught

"Marxism, with the active participation of millions, will usher in a new era in the United States. The great wealth of the U.S. will for the first time be used to benefit all people. Democrat-Socialist party granted

rights will be guaranteed and expanded. Racial, gender, and social equality will be the basis of all domestic policies and practices. Foreign policy will be based on mutual respect, peace, and solidarity. Marxism is not a dream but rather a necessity to improve working class people's lives and ensure the survival of developed human civilization. Only Marxism has the solutions to the problems of capitalism. The working class, the vast majority of the population, will have full political and economic power with Marxism. We, the working people of the United States, in order to form a more perfect union, need Marxism - a system based on people's needs, not on corporate greed. A radical critique of capitalism and the vision of Marxism form the basic ideas of the Democrat Party & the 'Communist Party, USA.'"

Marxism is what freedom is up against in 2020. Marxism is slavery in exchange for a false promise of utopia. In the end it is always about the same thing – control and money by elites. And that is why the Black Lives Matter militia wants all history to be erased; it has nothing to do with just the Confederacy. It has to do with erasing all history. Erasing history is the only way history can be repeated. That is why the monuments are being indiscriminately destroyed. It is the action that precedes all insurrections in history, and therefore must be erased. It is insanity allegiance in its purest form.

Americans – you are the majority. You can begin to form yourselves now or forever be under attack as individuals. The return of the 'Control-US-virus' this week is to isolate you. Begin to look for safety in numbers. Don't be isolated. Reach out. If your home is attacked, have a plan for your safety.

As General Flynn said, "2% of the passionate will control 98% of the indifferent 100% of the time if we don't wake up."

The reason many Americans have a hard time organizing to stop this mass hysteria is because we elect politicians to protect us from criminals. And when the politicians don't do their jobs, the system breaks down and revolutionaries can attack. Remember, when you hear the words Marxist or Democrat, the system is broken and it won't fix itself. Fix it now, or be fixed by the mob.

Marxism in the United States

At the dawn of the 21st Century, strong beliefs in Marxism became ubiquitous in the United States of America. There were four primary factors that caused this phenomenon to occur. The four are called, "The Marxist Kill Chain."

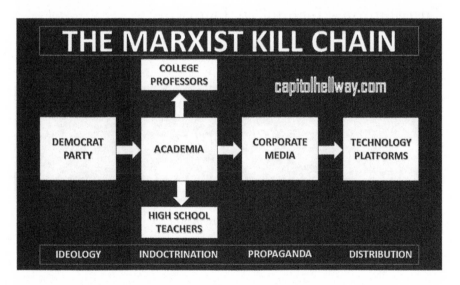

THE MARXIST KILL CHAIN

Ideology - Major Political Party

In 2020, it was the Democrat Party U.S.A.

Indoctrination - Academia

Colleges and universities, high schools and below.

Propaganda - Corporations / Media

The military industrial complex, Science Applications International Corporation, and corrupt corporate media, CNN.

Distribution - Technology Platforms

Google, Facebook and Twitter, and social media.

Free Advertisement

The Future of America

America After the 2024 Presidential Election

Washington D.C. - The U.S. stock market permanently closed today as Wall Street investors withdrew all investment capital from the global economy. The U.S., a former global superpower in the world, has a new government now.

President **Alexandria Ocasio-Cortez** today signed into law an Amendment to abolish the U.S. Constitution effective immediately.

The President published the new law using the hashtag #**newlaw** in a tweet this morning which says, *"The Constitution of the United States is hereby rescinded."*

 Alexandria Ocasio-Cortez ✓ @AOC

#newlaw

The Constitution of the United States is hereby rescinded. #newlaw

---

PUBLIC LAW 1

An Act

An amendment to the Constitution of the United States relative to terminating it.

That the following article is adopted as an amendment to the Constitution of the United States, which shall be valid to all intents and purposes as part of the Constitution:

Section 1. The Constitution of the United States is hereby rescinded.

APPROVED

Rashida Tlaib

Speaker of the House of Representatives

Ilhan Omar

Vice President of the United States and President of the Senate

Alexandria Ocasio-Cortez

President of the United States

The tweet contained this image of the new signed law.

Prior to making "its" announcement, the President was seen boarding the new space shuttle version of Air Force One. President Cortez has gone back and forth between sexes for years, and switched back again to self identify as a female in her first inauguration speech. There is no word yet whether she will change back to being a man now that she is a dictator, or begin referring to herself as some sort of hybrid like she did back in 2022, when she was the Secretary of State.

After the President's announcement, Vice President **Ilhan Omar** called the action *"A monumental achievement."* Then she said, *"I call on the entire nation to take to the streets and participate with all your other villagers in this historic event, our first mandatory national prayer to our new President."*

A spokesperson for Omar said that *armed prayer monitoring robots and drones* were being deployed by the FBI to all major population centers in the northeast and west coast. Meanwhile, volunteer armed militias still continued to battle the government backed Antifa Army in the south and across the mid-west. The government has had many problems with its weapons systems. For instance, last month *Resistance* forces hacked an entire squadron of government drones and a battalion of killer robots and attacked over 45,000 Antifa fighters in Detroit, Michigan. It was a blood bath, watching thousands of robots execute their own human fighters on

14

YouTube before the government shut it down.

Not to be outdone, former House Speaker **Rashida Tlaib**, who was appointed deputy vice-president under the new communist government, was entering her limousine when she was asked by a reporter from the China state run news agency whether the U.S. will have any elected representation.

> **Reporter:** "Your Excellency, with all due pardon to your highness and greatness, will the U.S. have elected representation?"

Tlaib responded with a loud grunt and pulled out her smartphone as she climbed into her limo surrounded by armed security guards.

A few moments later, she issued this statement on Twitter that bans all citizen input for everyone and imposes penalties for non-compliance.

"#newlaw – Effective immediately, all questions about citizen input are banned inside this country. Asking any questions about the government will result in imprisonment of 5 years or more."

 Rashida Tlaib ✔ @RashidaTlaib · 6m ⌄

#newlaw

Effective immediately, all questions about citizen input are banned inside this country. Asking any questions about the government will result in imprisonment of 5 years or more.

House Speaker Rashida Tlaib's sanity is a concern after a video from eight years ago surfaced. With her new power to block all citizen input, there is concern by *citizens* across all areas of the country that she may *"have to be dethroned,"* whatever that means.

In other news today, Gold hit a new high of $179 thousand dollars per ounce and sources close to the President say "it" is looking for a replacement currency for the U.S. dollar, and a replacement for the American flag.

WHAT YOU NEED TO KNOW

In a poll taken prior to the enactment of **Public Law 1**, 99.9 percent of all Americans said they supported *term limits for all members of Congress*. Asked in surveys why it was never enacted, all respondents said that they never called Congress to demand it back when they were free.

YOU CAN STOP ALL THIS FROM HAPPENING
CALL 202-224-3121
Ask to speak to your Senator
DEMAND THAT CONGRESS VOTE ON
H. J. RES. 20 & **S. J. RES. 1**
an amendment to the Constitution of the United States to limit the number of terms that a Member of Congress may serve

ANNOUNCEMENT: There will no longer be any new reporting on this page after this article is published. Government agents have rampaged our offices around the world and killed half our employees and their families. We don't know how many have been taken prisoner. Luckily, some of us escaped and we are joining the **RESISTANCE**. Semper Fi, Do or Die.

Behold the _key_ to all Knowledge for all time.

"THE MARXIST RABBIT HOLE"

inside Joe Biden's basement

BREAKING NEWS: Joe Biden held a news conference today to discuss his presidential debate preparations.

Some Americans say they are concerned about Joe Biden's stamina.

DEMOCRATS ARE BLAMING

JOE BIDEN
Entered Politics in 1970
47 YEARS
in Government

CHUCK SCHUMER
Entered Politics in 1975
45 YEARS
in Government

NANCY PELOSI
Entered Politics in 1987
33 YEARS
in Government

THIS GUY

DONALD J. TRUMP
Entered Politics in 2015
3.5 YEARS
in Government

FOR THE PROBLEMS
THEY CREATED

JOKE OF THE DAY

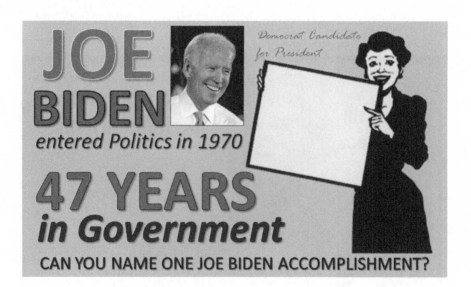

JOE BIDEN
entered Politics in 1970
47 YEARS in Government
CAN YOU NAME ONE JOE BIDEN ACCOMPLISHMENT?

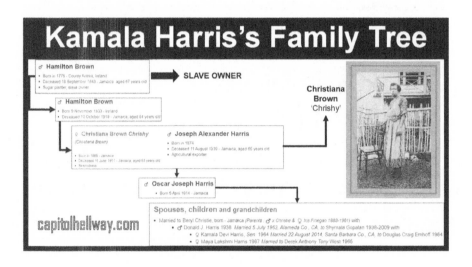

Capitol Hellway Media Company @CapitolHellway
QUESTION FOR Mr. VP @JoeBiden & @realDonaldTrump:
6/30/2020

Do you support the
#BlackLivesMatter
organization? It was founded by
Marxists. Does that concern you?

#545Rule300

BLACK LIVES MATTER

Patrisse Khan-Cullors
Co-Founder and Strategic Advisor

CO-FOUNDERS

"We are trained Marxists."

Alicia Garza
Co-Founder

MARXISTS

Support  Marxism

Public Service Announcement

Mike Yoder
@Yoder_Esqq Washington, D.C. instagram.com/yoder_esqq/

If you're arrested or fined for opening your business, not wearing a mask, or going to church, DM me.

I'll represent you for free.

2:23 AM · Jul 4, 2020 · Twitter for iPhone

capitolhellway.com

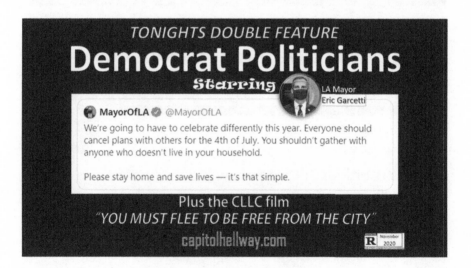

H. R. 6666

To authorize the Secretary of Health and Human Services to award grants to eligible entities to conduct diagnostic testing for COVID–19, and related activities such as contact tracing, through mobile health units and, as necessary, at individuals' residences, and for other purposes.

Free Advertisement

II

The Edwards "Knowledge Equation"

$$K=(q-a)/t$$

K=(q-a)/t

K=(q-a)/t

Knowledge equals the total sum of the thoughts and experiences between a question and its answer over time

*"Imagine that you spend your entire life in search of answers to questions that exist in your mind and no one else's. One day, you stumble upon the **key** to answering all your questions. That is the Knowledge equation in action. Knowledge is the **key** to the future of human life."*

John Stuart Edwards

The Two Functions of Time /t

"I think the periodic table of elements is the Garden of Eden."

John Stuart Edwards

$$K = (q-a)/t$$

The Knowledge Equation

All Time /t

Deity View - Now, and an hour from now. And yesterday, all at once.

Observed Time /t

Human View - Left and right. Up and down. What you know now.

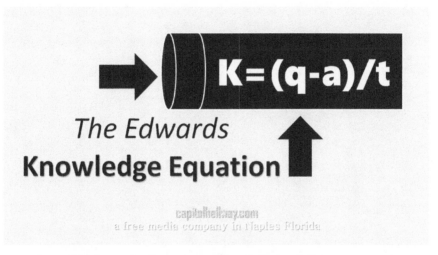

Petition to the Government for a Redress of Grievances

III

What are your frustrations? Here are some of mine.

Practice Session 2
Case Studies on Federal Government Corruption, Malfeasance and Reform

Amendment I
Congress shall make no law respecting an establishment of religion, or prohibiting the free exercise thereof; or abridging the freedom of speech, or of the press; or the right of the people peaceably to assemble, and to petition the government for a redress of grievances.

Death Penalty Needed For Government Corruption

On July 4, 1776, delegates from the 13 colonies adopted the *Declaration of Independence*, a historic document drafted by Thomas Jefferson that claimed independence from England and eventually led to the formation of the United States.

In 1870, the U.S. Congress made July 4th a federal holiday.

In the intervening years, politicians and corrupt career bureaucrats in Washington, D.C. and in states across the nation have selfishly diminished human freedoms and abused their authority. These scumbags regularly commit high crimes and treason against the United States under their own protection. They intentionally divide humans with the intent to conquer. They waste money and resources, and they retaliate against whistleblowers with impunity.

```
"I call on all readers of this story to tell the U.S. Congress
to pass laws that will kill Whistleblower Retaliators."
```

The Time for Justice Has Arrived!

"We must find creative ways to identify and then exterminate whistleblower retaliators if we are to remain a free and sovereign nation."

President Adams said, "Tyranny can scarcely be practised upon a virtuous and wise people."

"The time for action has arrived. Let us not continue to waste our independence with divisive and useless personal attacks that divide us. Instead, let's look to the future with hope by challenging our own characters and behaviors toward government corruption. Let us pledge to unite together under a declaration of war against the people who abuse their authority and eliminate them from our government by any means necessary."

Join the **Whistleblower Revolution** by sharing your stories about retaliation. We must identify all whistleblower retaliators so we can destroy them.

who do you believe should die?

Federal CIO Missing – Presumed Dead

A 52-year-old federal government *Chief Information Officer* was reported missing after his car was found abandoned in the parking lot of the Ilchester Elementary School near Baltimore on Thursday. Police investigators found splatters of blood on the steering wheel and windshield of the car and discovered a large blood trail leading to the road on the pavement nearby.

this is not real

Mangled body parts were also found a few blocks away on Montgomery Road in Maryland early today. Police have characterized the situation as "a dragging incident." The upper torso of the body was missing, and police believe the remains may have been torn apart and flung into a ditch somewhere along the road. Forensic teams are tracking the blood trails on the pavement to find the missing body parts and said they believe the dragging originated from the parking lot of the elementary school where the abandoned car was found.

The name of the missing bureaucrat has not been released. Earlier this month, a 56-year-old federal government bureaucrat and his wife were found beaten to death in their ransacked home. Police said that these two incidents may be related.

Howard County Police Department spokesperson Rancid Ass issued a statement saying that anyone with information about these crimes should call their anonymous tip line.

Corrupt Government Employee and Wife Found Slain

A 56-year-old federal government bureaucrat and his wife were found beaten to death in their ransacked home.

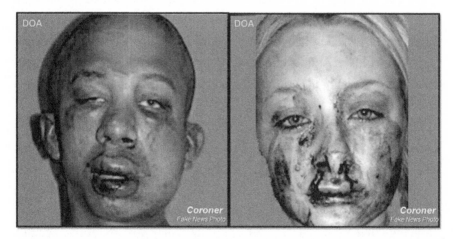

this is not real

The couple who resided at the 600 block of Sea Street in Washington D.C. had not been seen since they left work Friday, prompting a call to the police from a concerned co-worker late Monday night, according to investigators.

Police entered the couple's townhouse home at 1am Tuesday and found two severely bruised bodies in a bed. According to police Sergeant Bobby "Hoop" Middleman, the couple was beaten to death with a blunt object, but no weapon was found.

Although the home was in disarray, police were unable to say if anything was taken and the forensic team was unable to uncover any evidence linking a suspect to the murders. The names of the victims are being withheld pending notification of next of kin.

In a written statement, the police revealed that one of the victims may have worked at the National Labor Relations Board – *a.k.a. NLRB*, located at 1015 Half Street SE in Washington, D.C. based on a business card found near the scene.

Sergeant Hoop said that the African American male victim was accused of corruption and whistleblower retaliation and that his wife was Caucasian. Police also said both murders occurred on Friday evening, and that the whistleblower who was retaliated against was not a suspect. The spokesperson said that the whistleblower, whose name was being withheld from the press, was over one thousand miles away at the time of the murders drinking margaritas with friends on a beach. When questioned by the police, the whistleblower simply shouted, "Hooray," in a celebratory tone upon hearing the news about the murders, and then he took a big drink of tequila from a flask.

The spokesperson told reporters, "Our theory of the crime is that these murders were the result of a break-in gone bad," and added, "If anyone has any information about this crime, please call the MPD hotline."

One witness said she heard from some kids who were playing in the area that a man in a USPS delivery uniform visited the home on Friday night carrying what appeared to be a large rectangular box, about the size of a baseball bat.

Retaliation is What Government Bureaucrats Do

Fear no more the heat o' the sun;
Nor the furious winter's rages,
Thou thy worldly task hast done,
Home art gone, and ta'en thy wages;
Golden lads and girls all must,
As chimney sweepers come to dust.
Fear no more the frown of the great,
Thou art past the tyrant's stroke:
Care no more to clothe and eat;
To thee the reed is as the oak:
The sceptre, learning, physic, must
All follow this, and come to dust.
Fear no more the lightning-flash,
Nor the all-dread thunder-stone;
Fear not slander, censure rash;
Thou hast finished joy and moan;
All lovers young, all lovers must
Consign to thee, and come to dust.
No exorciser harm thee!
Nor no witchcraft charm thee!
Ghost unlaid forbear thee!
Nothing ill come near thee!

Quiet consummation have;
And renowned be thy grave!

The poem 'Fear no more heat o' the sun' by William Shakespeare is a poem about that death can come at any age, and all the troubles and worries happening while living will not matter while we are dead.

I am a Whistleblower

Nobody is ever held accountable in the U.S. government for breaking the law.

This letter was sent to Florida Congressman Mario Diaz-Balart, Senator Rick Scott and Senator Marco Rubio on September 29, 2019. Their response to this letter was swift, decisive and retaliatory.

On October 3 & 6 2019, the author of this letter received written death threats from Synta Keeling, a U.S. government official, in response to the letter. One month later on November 8, 2019, federal agents conducted a surprise attack on the family at their home to conduct an interrogation. Official complaints were filed with the FBI and ignored. Complaints were filed with the Council of the Inspectors General on Integrity and Efficiency for the illegal conduct of the Inspectors General involved, and illegal action was taken to cover up their misconduct.

Dear Member of Congress,

I am a **Whistleblower** who exposed billions of dollars in waste, fraud & abuse and other violations of the law in the U.S. federal government. My life was destroyed by the corrupt government officials named below.

I am writing to you today to provide a comprehensive simple solution to help all whistleblowers eliminate corruption in the government. There are six simple low-cost accountability steps that Congress can take now to protect all whistleblowers and eliminate government corruption.

DO YOU WANT TO HELP?

For blowing the whistle on corrupt government officials, I was retaliated against by:

The Special Assistant to President Trump Rosemary Lahasky & Labor Inspector General Scott Dahl Case# DC-1221-16-0227-W-1/ John Stuart Edwards v. Department of Labor.

The National Labor Relations Board Chief Information Officer Prem Aburvasamy & Inspector General David Berry Case# DC 0752-17-0467-I-1 / John Stuart Edwards v. National Labor Relations Board, and

The Department of Defense Inspector General Jon Rymer Case# 121468 / John Stuart Edwards v. SAIC.

All three of these Executive Branch Inspectors General committed high crimes and misdemeanors. It is blood-sport in the U.S. federal government today for corrupt bureaucrats to abuse the broken Freedom of Information Act and deceive the courts in order to bankrupt whistleblowers and destroy their lives.

Delay, deny, hope you die is the government's strategy to kill whistleblowing, and it works.

After a successful military and private sector career, I took a job as a data scientist to conduct investigative research inside the government. My job was to examine government operations and technologies to understand why the U.S. government costs so much to operate and help fix it.

For over 15 years, my field research would take me from the depths of the Pentagon to the Department of Home-land Security and Department of Labor and finally to the

National Labor Relations Board, a literal alphabet sou
government agencies.

In my work at the Department of Defense (DoD), my job was to assemble teams of data scientists and technologists to gain access to databases of all security classifications across the entire department with orders to create financial accountability.

In the history of the country, the DoD is the only organization in government that cannot pass a financial audit.

My whistleblower complaint to Inspector General Jon Rymer – Case# 121468 exposed major *Antideficiency Act* violations and fraud schemes carried out by contracting officers and executives and Board members at a major defense contractor including the former Secretary of Defense Robert Gates.

I uncovered billions of dollars in waste, fraud and abuse and cast sunshine on how they conceal their crimes by ensuring that the DoD never passes an audit. I blew the whistle on that beginning in 2010, and it is still happening.

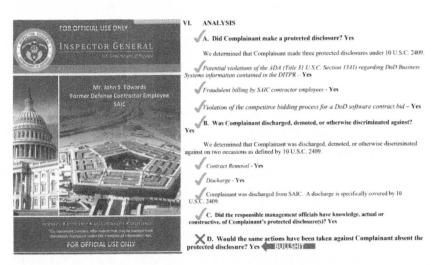

Findings of DoD Inspector General Whistleblower Reprisal Investigation

Here is proof of Bi-Partisan interest in this case in 2014.

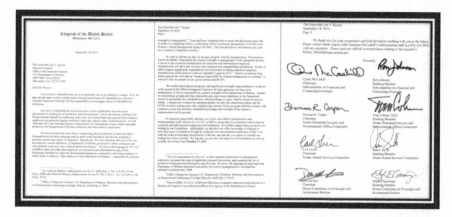

Bi-Partisan Letter signed by the Chairman & Ranking Members of the following Congressional Committees demanding that Inspector General Jon Rymer reverse his decision to vastly narrow my whistleblower protections in order to conceal crimes committed by the military industrial complex. Signatories included Senate Armed Services; House Armed Services; Senate Homeland Security & Governmental Affairs; House Government Oversight & Reform; and the Subcommittee on Financial & Contracting Oversight.

At the **Department of Homeland Security (DHS)**, I was the **Lead Modernization Architect** for the national **E-Verify system**. My job was to design and modernize that system for comprehensive immigration reform. My work was interrupted because Congress failed to pass comprehensive immigration reform. No matter. Anish and I left the system ready to scale. We both left the agency before we could be retaliated against after witnessing all the corruption going on there. Want to get to the 'true bottom' of corruption at **DHS**? Find out how often carpeting and office furniture is replaced, and work up from there. It's easy. The people with the most money to waste in government always flaunt it.

At the **Department of Labor (DOL)**, I was fired by former **Secretary of Labor Tom Perez** for reporting systemic discrimination against **African**

Americans. Here are two sentences from my testimony to give you a sense of the severity of his crimes.

"I swear before God that I personally witnessed eight highly competent African American federal employees be denied promotions and assignments that would enhance their careers. I was ordered to remain silent while a black woman was treated like a wild animal and herded into subservient jobs for many years because of the color of her skin."

Special Assistant to President Trump Rosemary Lahasky became involved in my case after her appointment by **President Trump** and she is carrying the torch to protect **Tom Perez** who went on to become the **Chairman of the Democrat National Committee**.

The **Department of Labor** case is still awaiting a quorum at the **Merit Systems Protection Board (MSPB).** The MSPB has been shut-down since **President Trump** took office in January 2017, because the **Senate** won't confirm **President Trump's** nominees. There are thousands of cases awaiting action now, and many of those cases are whistleblower complaints just like mine that could take many more years to be decided.

```
Delay, deny, hope you die is the government's strategy to kill
whistleblowing, and it works.
```

My whistleblower case against **Chief Information Officer Prem Aburvasamy & Inspector General David Berry** – Case# DC-0752-17-0467-I-1 was won in court in May 2017. I kicked their ass. Since that case closed, new evidence shows a clear nexus between the **Department of Labor** and the retaliation I suffered at the **NRLB** connecting the two. That evidence is going to be introduced in the **Rosemary Lahasky & Labor Inspector General Scott Dahl** case when it goes to trial. Oh. One more thing.

All three corrupt Inspector Generals have only one single thing in common. They were all appointed by President Barack Hussein Obama II.

DO YOU WANT TO HELP?

- **Confirm** nominees for the **Merit Systems Protection Board (MSPB)** and restore a quorum so cases may be heard.
- **Protect** whistleblowers who report fraud, waste and abuse by enacting legislation that guarantees reimbursement of all legal expenses for anyone who makes a protected whistleblower complaint in accordance with the law.
- **Punish** whistleblower retaliation by enacting legislation that makes retaliation a crime and imposes mandatory prison sentences for anyone in government convicted of whistleblower retaliation. If the person is a government contractor, the law should permit the government to cancel the contract.
- **Reform** the **Council of the Inspectors General on Integrity and Efficiency**—which oversees IGs at federal agencies by making it a crime to conceal lawlessness by its members.
- **Fix FOIA** by adding criminal penalties for violations of the **Freedom of Information Act** for government officials that illegally withhold information from the public or alter official records prior to release.
- **Vote for Term Limits** to end government corruption by calling an immediate vote for **Senate Joint Resolution 1** & **House Joint Resolution 20** to amend the **Constitution of the United States** to limit the number of terms that a Member of **Congress** may serve.

By taking these six simple low-cost accountability steps, **Congress** can restore dignity & respect to a government that has so much corruption today. If you don't act now, perhaps some future generation will read this and then they will know what to do, if we still have a country.

John Stuart Edwards
September 29, 2019

Ode To The Whistle-Blow

**THREE DAYS AFTER BEING ATTACKED AT OUR HOME BY
FEDERAL AGENTS, I WROTE THIS POEM**

~

Honor is discreet and helpless and wise,
The guardians – a system we despise,
Under cloak of darkness in the light rise,
The sound of the Whistle-Blow called a lie.

~

The people who know – recalcitrant fear,
No coming forward to hold what is dear,
Accusations and repudiations,
The sound of the Whistle-Blow hits deaf ear.

~

The Whistle-Blow is a very rare sound,
With so much corruption spinning around,
Evil bureaucrats dominate our lives,
The government, Washington, full of lies.

~

Money, corruption, and women who hide,
The truth is obvious before our eyes,
Yet darkness of shadow in the deep state,
Blocks honor and truth, heaven, and our faith.

~

Americans wake up! Stand up and rise,

Hear the Whistle-Blow sound, shout, come alive,
List retaliators who terrorize,
Unveil their retaliation disguise.

~

Disinfect corruptors with bright sun light,
Humiliate, torture, bankrupt their minds,
Bring to their families what they bring ours,
Cruelty, punishment, an eye for an eye.

~

Stand up, be bold, proud, and yell out your door,
"The time has come people, see the real world!"
Lock'em up, toss the key and publicize,
Put them in jail, humiliate, despise.

~

The boldness and power are what must die.
Their jobs, salaries, reputations, will –
Must be sacrificed, mutilated, killed.
To hear the sweet Whistle-Blow one more time.

~

Cruelness, temperament, tempered by steel,
Harshness, shameful, rules, obey make us kneel,
Take into our hands what government not,
The cipher of Whistle-Blow is red hot.

~

Ode to the Whistle-Blow, end the deceit,
Ode to the Whistle-Blow, hear us repeat,
Ode to the Whistle-Blow, it's a new time,
Ode to the Whistle-Blow, sunlight sunshine.

~~~

John Stuart Edwards

Systemic Racism Defined

"Systemic Racism" is present when the people in an organization at every level turn a blind eye to racism when it is presented to them. I would like to share my family's personal story about **Systemic Racism** in the U.S. federal government to demonstrate *how* it is permitted, approved and ignored by elected officials in both major political parties in Washington, D.C.

I was retaliated against by **Tom Perez**, the current Chair of the Democratic National Committee, for blowing the whistle on racial discrimination that was carried out against eight African Americans in 2015. Perez was previously Assistant Attorney General for Civil Rights (2009–2013) and United States Secretary of Labor (2013–2017) under former **President Obama** & **Vice President Joe Biden**. After my whistleblower retaliation lawsuit was filed, **President Trump** and his administration have ignored all my requests for help. In response to my whistleblower complaints to the White House, the Secretaries of Homeland Security, Labor & the Chairman of the National Labor Relations Board – all former employers of mine – have coordinated attacks against my family at our home. They dispatched federal agents on two occasions to interrogate me and intimidate my family. The controversial technique they used each time to circumvent a warrant is called "knock & talk." They just show up at your home without any prior notice. I recorded both of these encounters and filed official complaints each time with the FBI and Department of Justice, and nobody has followed up with me since.

The first attack happened on December 6, 2017, days after I first published this story. The second attack came in October 2019 in the form of death threat letters, and finally the third attack took place on November 8, 2019 against my family and our businesses in Naples, Florida. The Council of the Inspectors General on Integrity and Efficiency has taken no action against the Inspectors General involved and has taken affirmative steps to cover up their misconduct.

I contacted all the leaders of both political parties in Congress. My experience with my Congressman in Virginia is described below. After moving to Florida in August 2017, Republican **Congressman Mario Diaz-Balart** and Senators **Marco Rubio** and **Rick Scott** have ignored all our documented pleas and phone calls for protection. They have sanctioned the continuous threats to our lives, and the two "knock & talk" interrogations to intimidate my family. The mainstream media, including reporters at the *Washington Post* and *Bloomberg Law* may have ignored this case from the start for reasons that are not known to me.

> *__Tom Perez__, the current Chair of the Democratic National Committee is covering up systemic racism against eight African Americans. Eugene Scalia was sworn in as __Secretary of Labor__ on September 27, 2019, so he has the ball now and is just sitting on this case, hoping my time runs out. Hoping I die. And probably praying every night that this story doesn't pop out before the 2020 election. Tom Perez is banking on media silence because it involves the head of the DNC, and the GOP is riding his coattails by turning a blind eye to the systemic racism in plain sight that they refused to do anything about .*

Is that systemic enough for you? If not, please read on... you will be shocked at how systemic racism is permitted, approved and ignored by the bureaucrats inside the federal government, academia and the corrupt corporate media.

Below is a summary of my case. All filed court documents and motions and evidence are available upon request that demonstrate the entire federal government's unwillingness to expose racism at the Labor Department and the attacks they will make against anyone who does.

John Stuart Edwards v. U. S. Department of Labor docket number DC-1221-16-0227-W-1

MY TESTIMONY

> "I swear before God that I personally witnessed eight highly competent African American federal employees be denied promotions and assignments that would enhance their careers. I was ordered to remain silent while a black woman was treated like a wild animal and herded into subservient jobs for many years because of the color of her skin."

U.S. DEPARTMENT OF LABOR
EMPLOYMENT AND TRAINING ADMINISTRATION

John Stuart Edwards
Deputy Director
Office of Information Systems & Techology

200 Constitution Avenue NW
Washington, DC 20210

Telephone: (202) 693-3816
BlackBerry: (202) 465-1511
E-mail: edwards.john.s@dol.gov

INTRODUCTION

My name is John Stuart Edwards. I am a retired U.S. Marine Corps Mustang with a humble military and private sector career. My family has had our lives threatened by federal government employees because of what you are about to read and my case is still pending before the courts. As of Labor

Day 2020, it has been five years since I filed a whistleblower complaint and was dehumanized for wanting to stop discrimination against African Americans – and it is still not resolved.

Help! Help-Help! SOS. Mayday!

My objective in writing this story is to create a permanent digital record of the alleged unlawful acts of racism that I was ordered and refused to carry out while employed by the U.S. federal government with the hopes that one day justice will be served.

~ *I do hereby give my testimony standing on the shoulders of all the brave whistleblowers who came before me that know firsthand what it's like to lose everything after doing the right thing.*

JOHN STUART EDWARDS
WHISTLEBLOWER

FACT: I formally blew the whistle on systemic racial discrimination on behalf of eight African American employees that was being carried out by all senior executives and political appointees at the U.S. Department of Labor in Washington D.C. and I was retaliated against.

My case is still waiting to be heard by the courts.[1]

The decision by the courts in this case will transform government whistleblowing protections, forever. This case will drive a stake into the heart of Systemic Racism – if I can live long enough to have my day in court.

```
Delay, deny and hope you die is the government's strategy to
cover up Systemic Racism — and it works.
```

My complaint alleges that I received direct orders from my supervisor **Aung Htein** to actively discriminate against eight African Americans in the federal government who worked directly for me, and I was retaliated against – fired from my executive job – within days of refusing to execute those unlawful orders.

```
My case proves that the entire system of racial equality at the
United States Department of Labor is a farce.
```

THE LEGAL BATTLE DESCRIBED

The legal battle is against the United States Department of Labor whose legal position is that white people who report discrimination carried out by others are not protected from retaliation under federal Whistleblower Protection or Anti-Discrimination laws. [2]

Here is the essence of what happened to me:

58

I said to my boss, "I want to formally object to your order to
discriminate against eight African Americans who work for me,"
and then he said, "Nope, you cannot report discrimination of any
sort because you are a white male and furthermore, as punishment
for attempting to blow the whistle against me, you are fired!."

Indeed, my case is actually quite disturbing.

For anyone who wants to understand what it is like to navigate the
bureaucratic maze in order to uphold laws inside our government, this
article is for you. If you really want to know just how screwed up our
federal government really is, please read on.

"Systemic Racism" means that the people in an organization at
every level turn a blind eye to racism when it is presented to
them.

MY SYSTEMIC RACISM STORY

In 2015, I worked at the U.S. Department of Labor for **Aung Htein**, a
Burmese immigrant, who systemically carried out racial discrimination
for many years against African Americans; and I was retaliated against by
Aung Htein and his superiors and the entire Civil Rights establishment at

the Department of Labor for blowing the whistle to the Equal Employment Opportunity (EEO) office. Their collective vengeance against me and my family was swift, coordinated, destructive and has followed us since 2015, and two administrations.

Instead of firing Aung Htein for violating discrimination laws, I was fired for reporting his misconduct to authorities. After my firing, Aung Htein not only continues to be employed, he has been rewarded handsomely with bribes including skyrocketing pay raises, promotions and bonus payments to attend school.

Aung Htein (*born 1978*) is a career federal government bureaucrat whose taxpayer funded salary has skyrocketed despite continuous freezes on federal government pay. Mr. Htein's government salary has somehow miraculously grown from $115,000 in 2011, to over $183,000 per year today. That is a 60 percent pay raise at a time when there was supposed to be no federal pay increases at all. *But it gets even worse.*

In early 2017, Aung Htein was "mysteriously" promoted into the high paying ranks of the Senior Executive Service in the federal government – despite racial discrimination and retaliation complaints made against him that are still pending before the courts.

That's right. Aung Htein should have been fired. Instead, he was very generously compensated for keeping his mouth closed.

At the time of first publication for this article, Aung Htein was serving a one year probationary period which means he could have been terminated from the federal government immediately if action was taken to fire him. Unfortunately, his boss Rosemary Lahasky (Trump Appointee) refused to discipline Aung Htein and has protected him from prosecution.

RUMOR: Rosemary Lahasky is rumored to be a close associate of the President's daughter, Ivanka Trump, who is also a federal employee and works for her father. There is no evidence to support any rumors. React Research Respond

SHOW ME THE SYSTEMIC RACISM

I was Deputy Director and supervised fifty federal employees and over one hundred contractors at the Department of Labor technology office. My supervisor, Aung Htein, came into my office on September 1, 2015, and told me, *"to stop making noise,"* about the racial discrimination that he ordered me to carry out. Aung Htein told me that his bosses had promised him, "big pay raises and a promotion to the Senior Executive Service," at the U.S. Department of Labor for discriminating against African Americans.

I thought to myself at the time that this guy is clearly a racist, and I told Aung Htein that, "I will not participate in the discrimination of African American employees." After he left my office, I immediately notified his bosses – Lisa Lahrman and Byron Zuidema and setup meetings with them to report his misconduct. I was disappointed to learn how deeply they were involved.

After I exhausted my chain of command reporting the discrimination, Aung Htein took affirmative steps on September 15, 2015, to strip me of my supervisory responsibilities, remove my decision making authority and diminish my reputation. He announced to the entire office that I was no longer in charge of personnel decisions and that any complaints would need to be brought to him directly. This action made it clear to everyone in the office that if you fight for the rights of others, you will be humiliated and destroyed.

Just like we have seen recently in the news with victims of sexual assault, African Americans were discriminated against and afraid to come forward on their own. These Americans feared retaliation and they were right. I thought I could make a difference for them because I am white.

Looking back, I can understand now why these wonderful people refused to come forward on their own. Racists and sexual predators. The system allows them to behave and retaliate the same way. They have unlimited resources provided to them by large organizations, and it doesn't matter whether you are a man or a woman or black or white. If you stand up against power, if you make a complaint, everyone knows you will be destroyed. That is why people who witness discrimination and sexual harassment don't file complaints.

After the first retaliatory attack by Aung Htein and the lack of interest by his bosses to do anything about it, I filed a complaint with the U.S. Department of Labor Equal Employment Opportunity (EEO) Office and emailed copies of my complaint to Zachary Williams and Lisa Kyle who worked for (now former) Congressman Dave Brat (R-VA). At the time I resided in the Virginia 7th congressional district.

In my September 2015 EEO complaint, I wrote:

Allegations: Systemic discrimination against eight African American employees and retaliation for blowing the whistle to the entire Department of Labor leadership including the Inspector General.

Charge 1: Aung Htein and senior executives engaged in, and condoned racial discrimination to deny opportunities and career advancement for eight African American employees in the Department of Labor, Employment and Training Administration, Office of Information Systems and Technology. The following employees are current active targets of systemic discrimination by senior management officials that have or will directly impact the careers and earnings of these employees:

GS13 – Mr. McDaniel, an African American federal employee is being discriminated against because he is being denied a merit promotion solely due to his race. Mr. McDaniel applied for an advertised GS14 position to perform the work he is already performing at that level – and when Mr. McDaniel was found to be the only eligible qualified candidate and placed on the hiring certificate for the hiring official – *Aung Htein placed an indefinite delay on hiring Mr. McDaniel* for the position but has allowed the hiring of other vacant positions in the office, despite strong recommendations from the hiring officials including Mr. McDaniel's supervisor Thomas Flagg (also African American), the reviewing officer, and the Deputy Director.

At the time of the complaint, there was no indication whatsoever that Mr. McDaniel will ever have the opportunity to fill the position for which he is qualified. Mr. McDaniel stated that he feared retaliation if he filed an EEO complaint. [3]

GS13 – Mr. Liddell, an African American federal employee is actively being targeted by Aung Htein for removal from federal service despite the fact that Mr. Liddell is performing his work in a highly successful manner. This fact was corroborated by the senior GS15 technologists he supports, and his reviewing officer. Mr. Liddell's wife has been diagnosed with cancer and is undergoing chemotherapy treatments. Mr. Liddell has requested occasional time off to transport his wife to treatments. Mr. Htein stated that he considers these types of requests to be unsatisfactory and inappropriate. Mr. Liddell's supervisor, Freddie Sconce, stated in writing that he is acting to remove Mr. Liddell from federal employment based on his race on the orders provided to him by Aung Htein. Sconce stated that he disagreed with Mr. Htein's decision, but will carry out the orders despite his personal objections. Sconce, who was a GS-14, has applied for a GS-15 promotion and Aung Htein is now the deciding official for that promotion after the revocation of my personnel decision authority by Aung Htein on September 15, 2015.

In addition to the above active targets of discrimination, I uncovered a clear pattern of ongoing systemic discrimination that has been carried out for many years against only African Americans that were contained in my formal complaint and court documents. The following employees were also discriminated against and in some cases maliciously targeted and abused.[1]

- Ms. Marlene Howze
- Ms. Florence Davidson
- Mr. Thomas Flagg
- Mr. Kevin Jackson
- Mr. Dwayne Palmer
- Mr. Nat Brown

Charge 2: Aung Htein retaliated against me on September 15, 2015, when he removed my authority to manage personnel for reporting systemic discrimination to his superiors at the U.S. Department of Labor.

SYSTEMIC RACISM IS HELL

After a month passed, I became frustrated with a lack of response from EEO and the indifference by senior Department of Labor leaders concerning my complaints, so on October 13, 2015, I met with Vanessa Hall who is an EEO specialist and asked her advice about what I should do.

Ms. Hall said, "I have never seen or heard of a white executive coming forward to report racial discrimination against black people in my entire life. My experience is that they are going to keep coming after you if you keep complaining about what they have done [referring to Aung Htein, the Inspector General and Assistant Secretary of Labor]. You should probably just try to find another job."

Two weeks after meeting with Ms. Hall, I received an email permanently reassigning me to a non-supervisory Special Assistant position effective immediately. The new job was a made-up position that had never before existed, and it was not remotely commensurate with my senior management and supervisory experience and skills. The entire leadership of the Labor department was notified about the circumstances surrounding my reassignment, including the Inspector General and Zachary Williams who worked for Congressman Dave Brat (R-VA). None of them lifted a finger to help me then, or any time since.

From: Edwards, John S - ETA
Sent: Friday, October 30, 2015 2:01 PM

To: Htein, Aung - ETA; *Lu, Christopher P* - OSEC;
Zachary.williams@mail.house.gov; *Dahl, Scott* - OIG;
Wu, Portia - ETA; *Kerr, Michael* - ASAM; Colangelo, Matthew - OSEC;
Anderson, James - OASAM CRC; Hall, Vanessa H – ASAM
Kelly, Crystal L - ETA; Lewis, Sabrina M – ETA;

Subject: URGENT: EEO DISCRIMINATION AT ETA AND REQUEST FOR IMMEDIATE PROTECTION FROM REPRISAL

Sent: Thursday, October 29, 2015 3:32 PM
To: Edwards, John S – ETA

John,

Management has decided to reassign you. This reassignment will be effective Sunday, November 1, 2015. We have thoroughly reviewed your situation and have determined that this reassignment promotes the efficiency of the service.

You will retain your current office and report directly to Aung Htein.

Sincerely,
Lisa

A few days later, on November 5, 2015, my former Deputy Director position was advertised on the USAJOBS website as a vacant position to be filled.

After the reassignment and posting of my position, there was nothing for me to do but pay lawyers and fill out paperwork while I sat at home performing a bullshit job. In mid-November 2015, acting on the advice of my lawyer, I filed complaints with the Civil Rights Center and the Office of Special Counsel at the Department of Justice.

EDWARD C. HUGLER

RACIST

I made formal written complaints about discrimination against African American employees to *Betty Lopez* and *Naomi Barry-Perez* who run the Equal Employment Opportunity Office and Civil Rights Center at the Department of Labor. Betty Lopez admittedly reported my confidential EEO complaint to Edward Charles "Ed" Hugler who was the Deputy Assistant Secretary at Labor. She also informed the entire Department of

Labor executive team that I had filed a complaint about their discrimination and did nothing when I was retaliated against for making it. Hugler retired from the federal government after this story was first published.

On advice of my lawyer Peter Broida, I filed a complaint of Prohibited Personnel Practices (whistleblower reprisal) with the Office of Special Counsel (OSC) at the Justice Department, alleging that my reassignment to Special Assistant and the Labor department's decision to post my former position for hire, are retaliation for whistleblowing and for engaging in protected activities under 5 U.S.C 2302.

The OSC closed my whistleblower retaliation complaint without any investigation or followup on November 20, 2015, declining to seek corrective action on my behalf. Instead, they provided me with a right-to-file letter that day which stated that I needed to take my complaint instead to the Merit Systems Protection Board.[4]

NOT MY DEPARTMENT – TRY ANOTHER ONE

It became very clear that no one in the federal government has any interest in protecting African Americans against discrimination or protecting whistleblowers from retaliation.

Ka-Ching-Ka-Ching! Whistleblowers have to pay for all their legal representation while Aung Htein and his bosses are provided unlimited funding for government attorneys paid for entirely with taxpayer dollars. That is how the current system works. At the time of publication for this story, I have already spent approximately $20,000 on this case – and it is far from over.

Delay, deny, hope you die is the government's strategy to fight whistle-blowing, and it works.

BUT WAIT, IT GETS WORSE

Several months after I was removed from the position and replaced, there were several Inspector General complaints filed that allege Mr. Htein violated multiple sections of the Federal Acquisition Regulations, performed illegal acquisitions costing taxpayers millions of dollars, and accepted bribes and kick-backs from senior government officials in the form of personal training money totaling more than twenty thousand dollars in exchange for keeping his mouth shut about racism, corruption and whistleblower retaliation at the Department of Labor. Complaints were also made to the Inspector General about Aung Htein's pay raises and the promise he received about being promoted.

The Inspector General of the U.S. Department of Labor is Mr. Scott Dahl who was confirmed by the United States Senate on October 16, 2013. Dahl, who was appointed by President Obama, turned a blind eye to the discrimination and criminal complaints made against Aung Htein and other senior executives since he joined the agency. Dahl was part of the cadre of government executives at Labor who were involved in my reassignment and who have allowed Aung Htein to keep his job at the Department of Labor despite racism and criminal complaints.

After receiving an email request to comment on this chapter before publication after the death of George Floyd on May 25, 2020, Scott Dahl abruptly announced his retirement one week later on on June 3, 2020, with an effective date of June 21, 2020.

Aung Htein actively denied African Americans promotions and assignments that would enhance their careers. Htein used investigative services of the agency to target one African American woman, and he has been shielded from accountability by the Inspector General and government lawyers who are paid for by taxpayers to provide him with a free legal defense. Aung Htein has received substantial pay raises, and even been promoted to the highest ranks of the federal civil service.

HELLO? IS THERE ANYONE IN CHARGE?

Aung Htein's supervisor was Byron Zuidema, who was promoted to be the acting assistant secretary by President Trump. Zuidema abruptly resigned from the federal government after this story was first published despite expectations that he would remain in his new position for several more years.[5]

Rosemary Lahasky
RACIST

Rosemary Lahasky is another President Trump political appointee who is currently serving as the top White House official for the agency where Aung Htein works. Lahasky has experience working inside Washington D.C. as a congressional staffer but lacked the maturity, moral courage or experience to fire Aung Htein and put an end to his discriminatory ways after becoming involved in my case.

73

According to the Department of Labor website, Lahasky was the only person in charge of the Employment and Training Administration after Zuidema departed.[6]

EMPLOYMENT & TRAINING ADMINISTRATION (ETA)

Assistant Secretary	Vacant	(202) 693-2700
Deputy Assistant Secretary	Rosemary Lahasky	(202) 693-2700
Deputy Assistant Secretary	Vacant	(202) 693-2700

Rosemary Lahasky may also lack the authority to resolve this matter. I contacted her government funded attorney after moving to Florida in 2017, with an offer to settle this case and get on with my life. My offer stated, "Since I am retired now and so much time has already passed since my complaint was made, I am willing to consider agency demands for withdrawal of both cases – EEOC and MSBP – in exchange for reimbursement of my legal fees."

Here is the response I received to my offer. Rolando Valdez is the taxpayer funded full time government attorney who represents Lahasky and Htein. He works for the Department of Labor Solicitor.

Rosemary Lahasky was provided this story and offered no comment. *Capitol Hellway Media Company LLC* confirmed receipt by Ms. Lahasky of this article and our request for comment under the Freedom of Information Act – tracking number 847979.

-----Original Message-----
From: Valdez, Rolando - SOL
<Valdez.Rolando@dol.gov>
To: John Stuart Edwards
Sent: Fri, Oct 20, 2017 2:46 pm
Subject: RE: Settlement Offer

Dear John:

Thank you for this follow-up message. I did check
with ETA. They decline your offer and do not have a
counter-offer.

I recall that you have until March of 2018 to re-file
your EEOC case. I stand ready to proceed whenever
you decide to do so.

Sincerely,

Rolando Valdez

U.S. Department of Labor   Employment and Training Administration
200 Constitution Avenue, N.W.
Washington, D.C. 20210

January 18, 2018

John Stuart Edwards

RE: Freedom of Information Act (FOIA) Request
FOIA Tracking No. 847979

Dear Mr. Edwards:

This is in response to your Freedom of Information Act (FOIA) request dated December 27, 2017, and referred to the Employment and Training Administration (ETA), Office of Administrative Services (OAS) on December 29, 2017. Your request was assigned FOIA Tracking No. 847979. You requested a copy of the following email that was received by the email address of Deputy Assistant Secretary Rosemary Lahasky, email account lahasky.rosemary@dol.gov or affiliated Department of Labor system or network aliases for Ms. Rosemary Lahasky dated December 20, 2017, between 7:00-9:00 p.m.

We conducted a search for responsive documents, both hard-copy and electronic, and located one page, responsive to your request. After reviewing these records, we have determined that the records can be released in their entirety.

In accordance with Department Regulations, 29 C.F.R. § 70.43, the charge for this material, which would have been *de minimis*, is waived.

If you need further assistance or would like to discuss any aspect of your request, you may contact Maria Sanders, ETA's FOIA Program Manager at 202-693-3101 or DOL's FOIA Public Liaison:

Mr. Thomas Hicks, Esq.
FOIA Public Liaison
U.S. Department of Labor
Office of the Solicitor
Management and Administrative Legal Services
Office of Information Services
200 Constitution Avenue, N.W.
Room N-2420
Washington, D.C. 20210
Phone: 202-693-5427
Email: Hicks.Thomas@dol.gov

Lahasky, Rosemary - ETA

From:	CapitolHellway . <capitolhellway@gmail.com>
Sent:	Wednesday, December 20, 2017 7:46 PM
To:	Lahasky, Rosemary - ETA
Subject:	Rosemary Lahasky is in the news!

Good evening Ms. Lahasky, I just published a story about discrimination against African Americans at your agency.
Would you like to comment? If so, please text or call me at ▮▮▮▮▮▮ at a convenient time.

Read article:

Aung Htein Terrorized African Americans at Labor Department

Congratulations on your recent promotion from Chief of Staff to Deputy Assistant Secretary. That is quiet a bump in pay.
Have a wonderful holiday and Merry Christmas!

Warmest Regards,

John Stuart Edwards

Journalist

After reporting her malfeasance to the White House numerous times, Rosemary Lahasky – instead of being disciplined & fired – was promoted by President Trump to be Special Assistant to President Trump and Director of Domestic Initiatives – Office of Economic Initiatives on April 12, 2019.

```
RUMOR: In her new role, Rosemary Lahasky is rumored to work
closely with and be under the protection of the President's
daughter, Ivanka Trump, working on job training grant programs
for the administration. There is no evidence to support any
rumors. React Research Respond
```

My complaint was about Rosemary Lahasky's knowledge of the systemic racism that I reported to her, and the fact that she took no action to correct it.

```
"Systemic Racism" is present when the people in an organization
at every level turn a blind eye to racism when it is presented
to them.
```

Rosemary Lahasky sits at the big table of systemic racists working for the United States federal government. It is a national protection network.

*The Whistleblower retaliation component of this case is still await-ing action by the U.S. Merit Systems Protection Board that has lacked a quorum since President Trump took office in 2017. **This precedent setting case will establish whether white people who report discrimination carried out against African Americans are protected from retaliation under federal law.** Unfortunately, since the* Merit Systems Protection Board *lacks a quorum because President Trump and the Republican controlled Senate refuse to fill the vacancies – and no reporter will demand that they answer why these vacancies remain and the impact of that on whistleblowers, there is a backlog of thousands of cases building and it could be many more years – or even decades – before my case is resolved. Here is how they get away with it.*

TAXPAYER FUNDED LEGAL DEFENSE FOR RACISTS

News reports have already revealed that Congress secretly paid out settlements of over $17 million for discrimination, sexual assault and other cases brought against Members of Congress.

What Americans don't know is that every department in the federal government operates exactly the same way as Congress but with much larger budgets. Each agency and department of the government has its own secret slush fund to pay lawyers and settlements that they hide from public view.

Here is the reason why we know so little about that money.

The perpetrators of racial discrimination and retaliation at the Department of Labor know they cannot be sued as individuals because they have immunity, so the agency gets sued. In my case, I'm suing the Department of Labor, but it is Taxpayers who end up paying the bill. And that is how the system is rigged. Bureaucrats have billions of dollars in their budgets and an unlimited amount of time – in many cases their entire career – to sit at a government desk with a government computer and fight against anyone who stands against them, and they know it.

This is true for every federal agency whether IRS, EPA or any other number of departments in the bureaucratic sphere.

And the Department of Labor is no different. Aung Htein and Rosemary Lahasky don't care about lawsuits against the agency because taxpayers fully fund a large federal legal department to protect them. The Department of Labor is packed with government lawyers, like Rolando Valdez, that are funded by taxpayers to defend the people who discriminate against African Americans and retaliate against Whistleblowers. *The entire system is upside down.*

Nicholas C. Geale, was appointed Acting Solicitor of Labor by President Trump on February 17, 2017, and also served as the Chief of Staff for the former Secretary of Labor R. Alexander Acosta.

Geale was responsible for providing free legal advice, representation and trial services for government executives who break the law. His office is still defending Aung Htein and representing Rosemary Lahasky, who are now working together to cover up discrimination, sexual assault and Whistleblower retaliation at the Department of Labor. All this legal support is provided at taxpayer expense. And Geale and Rolando Valdez have a much larger budget to work with than anyone who makes a complaint against the agency.

Delay, deny, hope you die is the motto there.

Nicholas Geale abruptly departed the government in mid-2019 after a White House investigation into complaints about mistreating staff and misleading Trump administration personnel. The announcement came after a White House Office of Management and Budget investigation into complaints that Geale cultivated a threatening, hostile work environment and misled White House staff about progress on Labor policies.

NICHOLAS GEALE

RACIST

CONGRESS IS USELESS

In 2015, I lived in the Virginia 7th congressional district. According to federal law, Whistleblowers who report retaliation to Congress are supposed to be protected. I have dozens of communications back and forth with Congressman Dave Brat's office spanning more than ten months, and he did not lift a finger to help.

In January 2016, I was becoming frustrated by the lack of interest in my case by Congressman Dave Brat's staff.

-----Original Message-----
From: John Stuart Edwards
To: Lisa.Kyle <Lisa.Kyle@mail.house.gov>
Sent: Thu, Jan 21, 2016 11:33 am
Subject: Re: Casework

Lisa,

I have not received a response from you and we have passed 90 days and $15k in legal fees since I first contacted the Congressman's office for help. On Nov 18, you said "It may take 30 days before I receive a reply." Do you have an update for me please. If not, can you let me know?

I have never met Congressman Brat but I do know he talks about corruption in Washington on the news, but he needs to know that Whistleblowers are being punished in his district by the bureaucracy up there, and honestly I am starting to believe he doesn't care about that. I sure hope I'm wrong about that.

This is all going to become public at some point.

Thank you.
John Stuart Edwards

Every month in 2016, I contacted Congressman Brat's office and kept getting the same response, "As soon as we receive a reply, we will update you." Month after month after month passed by, and nothing was being done. In August 2016, I was so frustrated that I sent Congressman Brat this email and never got a response or call from his office again.

-----Original Message-----
From: John Stuart Edwards
To: Lisa.Kyle <Lisa.Kyle@mail.house.gov>
Sent: Mon, Aug 15, 2016 8:13 pm
Subject: Re: Case Update

Tell the congressman he is useless and instead of spending all his time posting conservative BS on his Facebook page tell him he should get off his behind and serve his constituents. You people are pathetic and have no clue what it is like to fight for your country. You're too busy trying to keep your jobs. Another Cantor. All talk no action.

John Stuart Edwards

I guess he was offended. It was a big mistake for me to think that anyone in Congress would do the right thing. Dave Brat was just like all the others who go to Washington and ignore their constituents. They enter the swamp and become corrupted. Dave Brat lost his reelection bid in a solidly Republican district to a Democrat in 2018, because, like his predecessor Eric Cantor – he got corrupted when he went to Washington D.C.

FIRE AUNG HTEIN!

Clearly the most important qualification for promotion into the federal government's Senior Executive Service at the Frances Perkins Building in Washington, D.C. is to discriminate against African Americans and retaliate against any federal employee or contractor who blows the whistle on illegal activity there.

I experienced a horrible tragedy and injustice when I reported the discrimination of African American employees at the Department of Labor, and was retaliated against for opening my mouth. The eight African American employees that I stood up for have suffered the most.

If you are an African American who worked at the U.S. Labor department since it was founded on March 4, 1913, chances are you were discriminated against or feared retaliation if you filed a complaint against your supervisors during your employment there. That is Systemic Racism, and this article has explained how it is defined.

NOTES

1.**From:** Edwards, John S – ETA
Sent: Wednesday, October 28, 2015 8:53 AM
To: Zuidema, Byron – ETA <Zuidema.Byron@dol.gov>; Lahrman, Lisa L. – ETA <Lahrman.Lisa.L@dol.gov>; Htein, Aung – ETA <Htein.Aung@dol.gov>
Subject: RE: Update
Lisa and Byron, thank you for scheduling and meeting with me to follow up on this email yesterday. As I stated in the meeting to you both, I feel it is important for me to stay on and support the ongoing EEO investigation resulting from my initial claims so I will stay in my current position as deputy director in OIST until the dust settles on that before considering any other positions.

I look forward implementing WIOA during this next year!

John

2. See Equal Employment Opportunity Commission case number 570-2016-01154X / Agency No. 16-11-021 / and U.S. Merit Systems Protection Board, docket number DC-1221-16-0227-W-1 / John Stuart Edwards v. U. S. Department of Labor for case documents and material evidence to substantiate all allegations against named individuals in this article.

3. One year after this complaint was filed; Mr. McDaniel stated in an email that he was unceremoniously promoted to the GS-14 grade as a result of this complaint and he thanked me for standing up for his rights.

4. See U.S. Merit Systems Protection Board, docket number DC-1221-16-

0227-W-1 / John S. Edwards v. Department of Labor / for case documents and material evidence to substantiate all allegations against named individuals in this article.

5. *See Department of Labor Agency Case Number CRC 16-11-021 dated May 8, 2018* **FINAL AGENCY DECISION** *page 8 paragraph 2, page 9 paragraph 3,* **and** *page 11 paragraph 2, for contradictory testimony (lies) from Lisa Lahrman & Aung Htein about the reason that I was removed.* **AA (Lahrman) attested Complainant did not inform her at any time** *that he no longer wanted to leave OIST-ETA until her meeting with him on October 27, 2015 (see footnote 1).* **Director1 (Htein) testified he became aware of Complainant openly opposing discrimination on October 30, 2015 and that he did not become aware of the EEO complaint until February 15, 2016.** *DAS (Zuidema) testified, on October 10, 2015, Complainant sent an email to him, AA (Lahrman), and Director1 (Htein) stating,* "*I will stay in my current position.*" *(Tab Affidavit D, p5). DAS testified that he did not know if the October 10, 2015, email was considered prior to reassigning Complainant. Also see multiple emails – i.e. Footnote 1 –* **that prove that the removal was retaliatory and Director1 (Htein) lied in his testimony about the dates he knew about the EEO complaint.**

6. Update – Molly E. Conway, Phone (202) 693-2772 was appointed Acting Assistant Secretary in 2018.

Climate Change for Dummies

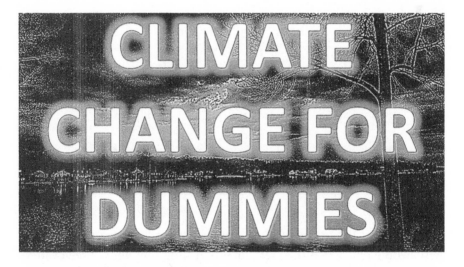

**POLITICIANS SAY THEY CAN CHANGE THE WEATHER
ARE YOU A BELIEVER?**

The purpose of this article is to explain why **"Climate Change"** is a threat to human existence on earth and what rational people in the world can do about it.

Climate Change is a change in global or regional climate patterns. According to NASA,[1] the Earth's climate has changed throughout history. For example, in the last 650,000 years there have been seven cycles of glacial advance (cooling) and retreat (warming), with the end of the last major ice age occurring about 11,000 years ago.[2]

The effects of changes in global or regional climate patterns can be very significant. For example, the Sahara is a desert located on the African continent. It is the largest hot desert in the entire world today. Its area is comparable to the total land mass of China or the United States.[3] At the end of the last ice age, it was a desert.

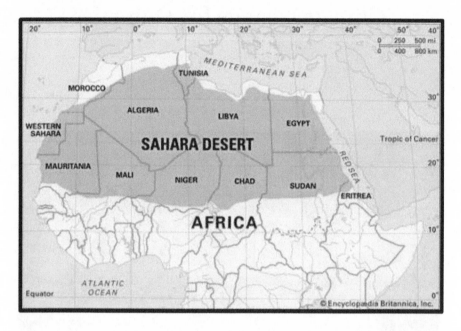

However, after the last ice age the Sahara Desert became lush and populated with people that established settlements around rain pools, green valleys, and rivers. According to the Journal of Science, around 10,500 years ago, a sudden burst of monsoon rains over the vast desert lasting a few hundred years transformed the region into habitable land for more than 5,000 years. This opened the door for humans to migrate into the area, as evidenced by radiocarbon dates of human and animal remains from more than 150 excavation sites. After many millennia, the rains ended and the Sahara returned to desert conditions which coincides with major population migrations into the Nile Valley and the formation of pharaonic society.[4]

These changes in climate to the Sahara and throughout history are attributed to very small variations in the Earth's orbit that changed the amount of solar energy our planet receives. In an analysis of the past 1.2 million years, geologists examining ocean sediment cores have discovered a pattern that connects the regular changes of Earth's orbital cycle to changes in the Earth's climate.[5]

Now that we know how solar energy can dramatically alter the climate of massive regions on the globe by turning the Sahara into gardens and back again into a desert over thousands of years, let's turn our attention to the other factors that can influence the earth's ability to retain the solar energy it receives from the sun.

CO_2 is a colorless gas that consists of a carbon atom bonded to two oxygen atoms. CO_2 occurs naturally in Earth's atmosphere and has many natural sources. Because carbon dioxide is soluble in water, it occurs naturally in groundwater, rivers and lakes, ice caps, glaciers and seawater. It is also present in deposits of petroleum and natural gas.[6]

CO_2 gives life. One of the first things taught in biology class is that animals breathe in oxygen and exhale CO_2, while plants take in CO_2 and release oxygen.

In a process called "photosynthesis," plants use the energy in sunlight to convert CO_2 and water into sugar and oxygen. The plants use the sugar for food – food that we use, too, when we eat plants or animals that have eaten plants – and they release the oxygen into the atmosphere. If it were not for plants, we would have no oxygen in our air.[7]

About 99% of the earth's atmosphere consists of nitrogen and oxygen and the remaining 1% contains several trace gases, including Carbon dioxide (CO_2), whose current concentration represents just 0.04% of the atmosphere, or 400 molecules out of every million which is **400 parts per million** – or as scientists say, 400 ppm.[8]

In other words, about 99.96 percent of today's atmosphere is not CO2.

From a historical perspective, an atmospheric CO_2 concentration of 400 ppm is almost scraping the bottom of the barrel. Over the Earth's history, atmospheric CO_2 concentrations have ranged from 182 ppm to 7000 ppm.

On that scale we are in fact today barely above the Earth's record lows.[9]

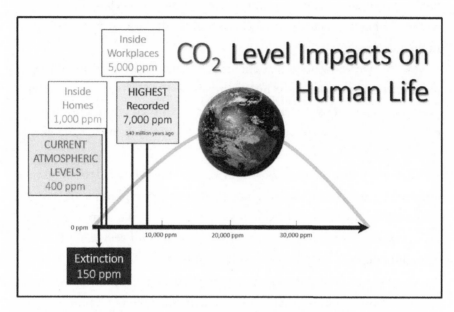

To fully understand CO_2 levels and its impact on human life, consider that at the end of the last ice age, CO_2 fell to 182 ppm (compared to 400 ppm today) which is thought to be the lowest in the Earth's history. If CO_2 drops below 150 ppm, most terrestrial plant life cannot exist.[10]

At the other end of the spectrum, CO_2 levels of 400 to 1,000 ppm are typically found in occupied spaces (homes) with good air exchange, and levels up to 5000 ppm is the permissible daily workplace exposure limit in most jurisdictions. Exposure to CO_2 levels above 40,000 ppm can lead to serious oxygen deprivation resulting in permanent brain damage, coma, even death.[11]

CO_2 and other gases may also influence the earth's ability to retain the solar energy it receives. The mechanism by which carbon dioxide traps heat in the atmosphere is commonly referred to as the **"Greenhouse Effect."** Stated very simply, this theory says CO_2 is nearly transparent to the solar radiation emitted from the sun, but partially opaque to the thermal radiation emitted by the earth. As such, it allows incoming solar radiation from the sun to pass through it and warm the earth's surface. The earth's surface, in turn, emits a portion of this energy upwards toward space as thermal radiation. Some of this thermal radiation is absorbed and re-radiated by the atmosphere's CO_2 molecules or other gases back toward earth's surface, providing an additional source of heat energy that causes temperatures to rise. Without CO_2 in the air, all plant life would die and the Earth's average temperature would be about **94°F cooler** than it is today.[12]

Without CO2, the entire United States and the rest of the globe could be thrust into an ice age from which there may be no return.

Now, there is very little substantive dispute among scientists and earth practitioners that the current use of fossil fuels such as coal, oil and gasoline releases large amounts CO_2 into the Earth's atmosphere and oceans. This recent "human-made" phenomenon of fossil fuel use has increased significantly in the last 100 years due to global population growth, industrialization and war. While many of the effects have been mitigated by regulations, the recent uptick in global CO_2 has been significant.

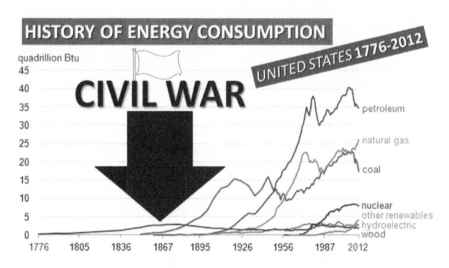

Global climate activists fueled by some politicians insist that "human-made" fossil fuel use will end civilization in this century or the next if draconian measures are not taken to curb fossil fuel use in the United

States and around the world. "Green New Deal" legislation is showing up in federal and state legislatures around the globe to enact a variety of measures intended to curb CO_2 emissions created by humans (and in some cases livestock). These proposals are far reaching but do contain some commonsense solutions, such as helping communities affected by **Climate Change**, upgrading existing infrastructure to withstand extreme weather and investing in renewable power sources.[13]

Critics of plans like the "Green New Deal" tend to overlook the commonsense solutions and highlight the more radical aspects of some of the proposals that they feel are unimplementable. As a result, the issue of **Climate Change** has become a political football that, like most things politicians touch, turns to shit.

```
And that is precisely the issue. On the one hand, there is
universal scientific agreement that "Climate Change" is
inevitable. Remember the Sahara Desert example above? It is a
fact that the climate of this planet is changing just like it
has done since the beginning of time.
```

On the other hand, global climate activists believe that the increases in CO_2 from "human-made" fossil fuel use is rapidly accelerating the Earth's decline. These activists along with their politicians portend that higher levels of CO_2 caused by "human-made" fossil fuel use is the primary cause of ice caps melting, sea levels rising, forest fires and intense storms.

This is where their argument breaks down. First of all, let's look at this logically. Do you believe that the earth is so fragile that humans can do to the climate – in just a few years – what science tells us takes nature hundreds of thousands of years to do?

Climate activists and politicians are acting out a scene from a science fiction movie where pollution loving mad scientists are threatening to destroy the world with weather-changing machines that emit CO_2 into the atmosphere. And unless all the people on the planet relinquish their rights, end capitalism and turn over all their treasure as ransom, we are all going to die.

*This is known as the "**Climate Change Hoax**" and its purpose is to create mass hysteria leading to "**Mob Rule**" and global government.*

Mob Rule is defined as the control of a political situation by those outside the conventional or lawful realm, typically involving violence and intimidation.

Look around. See what they say, see what they do. Do I really need to say anymore?

In fact, if you were to plot average global temperatures and atmospheric CO_2 concentrations over the past 550 millennia (thousands of years), derivable from glacier ice cores and marine sediments, you would see that approximately 540 million years ago, carbon dioxide in the air peaked at almost 7,000 parts per million – more than 17 times today's level. Yet even at that high level, average temperatures at the time were only about 22°C (71.6°F). Rather than being detrimental to life, this peak in atmospheric CO_2 coincided with the greatest eruption of life the Earth has ever experienced: the **Cambrian Explosion**.[14] During this time, almost all the modern plant and animal phyla we know today arose. Since then, CO_2 concentrations have followed almost a straight line downwards. Our current increases in atmospheric carbon dioxide are only a very short-term, unobservable blip on this very long-term record.[15]

The key to addressing **Climate Change** – which is inevitable, is for Americans to educate themselves on the causes we don't control – Earth's orbit, and let innovation through capitalism create demand for solutions to the problems we do control – fossil fuel use.

As you can see, the **Climate Change** problem is not binary. It doesn't have to be a choice between the extreme point of view that the world will end by 2030 if we don't abandon capitalism, or believing that **Climate Change** doesn't exist. There is a rational middle ground.

To wrap this up, here are *four actions* to consider that the United States could take to address the coming climate problem. This article has explained why the climate is going to change and that human fossil fuel use is adding CO_2 which can increase temperatures. Whether you believe "human-made" fossil fuel use is accelerating the Earth's decline or not – we should be able to agree – based on science and history – that the **Climate Change** phenomenon is real, and that if we don't begin to address it at some point – **Climate Change** will cause massive migrations by future generations of humans, and possibly cause the total extinction of our species from the face of the earth.

We Need Commonsense Solutions

The four actions that Americans can take to combat Climate Change are:

Ignore Washington D.C. Politicians – *"We The People"* in the United States are 26.5 trillion dollars in debt and that debt is growing exponentially by the second. Twenty U.S. veterans commit suicide each day. Social Security, Medicare and Medicaid are going bankrupt, healthcare costs are skyrocketing, infrastructure is crumbling, and we have a border crisis, and homelessness & crime that are devouring our cities. If the politicians can't work together to fix these comparatively simple problems, how in the hell are they going to change the weather?

De-politicize Climate Change Education – By focusing almost exclusively on the impacts of "human-made" fossil fuels on the environment in school curriculums and not the orbital or other terrestrial causes of **Climate Change**, the United States has created an entire generation of citizens who are not fully informed. It's like teaching only creationism or evolution and not both. The result is imbalance, which causes irrational fear and emotion to drive decisions instead of commonsense. When it comes to the existence of life on Earth, humans need to feed our minds with the full picture of thought – and stop acting like a mob! We need balance and reason in **Climate Change** education, not the endless propaganda and fear we see in the media today.

Stimulate Free-Market Demand for Climate Survivability – We subsidize trains, we subsidize planes, and we subsidize corporations... why not subsidize the continued existence of people? Each year the United States appropriates "Emergency Aid Bills" to help communities devastated by that day's catastrophic event, but we do nothing to prevent them from happening. For what the U.S. spends on emergencies each year, it could begin making incremental investments by matching the disaster aid amounts in order to upgrade existing infrastructure in areas known to be at risk to **Climate Change** so those communities can withstand extreme weather.

Become a multi-planetary species – We live in a very complex universe that is constantly changing and humans have all been blessed by God with incredible minds and technology. The global threats that humans have created – terrorism and nuclear apocalypse, barely scratches the surface of what nature can do to us. One day, whether it's **Climate Change**, a large meteor strike, a massive shift in the Earth's orbit, or even a solar anomaly – our days on this planet are probably numbered. Elon Musk captured the essence of this best when he said,

> "I think there is a strong humanitarian argument for making life multi-planetary, in order to safeguard the existence of humanity in the event that something catastrophic were to happen, in which case being poor or having a disease would be irrelevant, because humanity would be extinct. It would be like, 'Good news, the problems of poverty and disease have been solved, but the bad news is there aren't any humans left.'[16]"

The primary role of government in **Climate Change** should be to ensure that its citizens have access to the information and shared resources needed to safely mitigate the impacts of changes to the weather, and help society replenish itself after significant weather events.

If we can all agree that **Climate Change** is real and ultimately poses a threat to humanity – which it does, then I think we can begin to take the rational steps needed as humans in a civilized society to ensure the continued survivability of the human race and its freedom for all time.[17]

After all, do you really believe politicians can change the weather?

The below fake news article represents how the climate change issue is viewed by many Americans because politicians claim they can control the weather. Not everyone believes they can, and that is not unreasonable.

BREAKING NEWS – CLIMATE CHANGE MEETINGS HELD TODAY

"A gathering of the *Climate Mob* was held in more than 1,000 locations in the United States today to protest the fast approaching end of the world. *Climate Mob* fanaticism is a religious cult perfected by the freaks in the Democrat party in the early 21st century to infiltrate and sabotage the U.S. government.

Irrational fear and belief in an imminent climate catastrophe has steadily gained popularity in the U.S. among the mainstream media elite and college students who expect to have $1.5 Trillion in student loan debt paid off by taxpayers in exchange for supporting the radical *Climate Mob* agenda.

Followers of the *Climate Mob* are conditioned by their Democrat party handlers to have *Pavlovian* responses to media reports that act as 'triggers' to invoke specific group clinical psychotic behavior. For example, participants at today's *Climate Mob* gatherings are being conditioned to demand total government control over every aspect of human life including birth, health, nutrition and the right to own firearms for personal protection. There is nothing sane about demanding that the government control all of human life under *Climate Mob* rule.

The capability to use mind control to cause psychotic behavior on a large scale is also being perfected by social media companies under the tutelage of the Democrat party for the 2020 election. By any measure of sanity, the *Climate Mob* is nothing more than a collection of malcontents and losers that have lost their minds to a political party. As a result, today's gatherings of the *Climate Mob* represent the largest national organized event for the clinically insane since the 2016 Democrat national convention and the greatest threat to freedom in America since the Civil War."

About the author – I am not an earth scientist. I am an educated and informed American citizen that is fed-up with the propaganda of special interest groups, academics, corrupt corporate media and politicians who are taking advantage of some citizens by using extreme threats of imminent catastrophic climate destruction to gain power and total control over our lives at a time when we should be solving the immediate problems that threaten our safety and quality of life on this planet. *Community ecosystems in the United States can become environmentally secure.* I believe they can.

NOTES

1. Source "Climate Change: How Do We Know?"

2. According to some research, at least five of the seven climate cycles were major ice ages.

3. Source: Wikipedia

4. Source: "Sahara Desert Was Once Lush and Populated"

5. Source: "Geologist connects regular changes of Earth's orbital cycle to changes in climate"

6. Source: Wikipedia

7. Source: "Plants need CO2 to live"

8. Source: "Climate Science Investigations"

9. Source: "Atmospheric CO2 Concentrations At 400 PPM Are Still Dangerously Low For Life On Earth"

10. Source: Wrightstone, Gregory. INCONVENIENT FACTS: The science that Al Gore doesn't want you to know . Mill City Press. Kindle Edition.

11. Sources: "Carbon Dioxide Detection and Indoor Air Quality Control" and "What are safe levels of CO2?"

12. Source: "CO_2 Science" and "Heat-Trapping Effects of CO2 Measured in Nature for First Time"

13. Source: "The Green New Deal Explained"

14. See Cambrian explosion

15. Source: "CO2 Levels In Air Dangerously Low for Life on Earth"

16. Source: "In Order to Ensure Our Survival, We Must Become a Multi-Planetary Species"

17. If any source in this article is inadvertently omitted or incorrect, please contact me so that I may issue a correction.

My Manifesto

My Manifesto is an instruction manual to save the world from government tyranny fueled by greed and the military industrial complex.

PREAMBLE -Manifesto

The Secretary of Defense at the time was **Robert Gates**, Chancellor of the *College of William & Mary*, who 'coincidentally' was a member of the SAIC Board of Directors prior to being appointed to be the **Secretary of Defense** by two Presidents, who 'coincidentally' came from each major political party. This man believes the military should run the earth.[1]

Republicans and Democrats are all corrupt. We are being asked to choose between two worsts. Every decision politicians make has money behind it. In my experience, all people on the inside of an organization who steal have an incentive to cover it up. It is no different in the government.

```
People steal, and they work together to cover it up.
```

In my work at DoD, my job was to assemble teams of data scientists and gain access to databases of all security classifications across the entire department with orders to create financial accountability. In the history of the country, the DoD is the only organization in government that says it cannot pass an audit, so it never gets audited. Pretty sweet deal if you can keep it.

In my job at the Pentagon, I had access to classified data about nuclear subs, stealth aircraft, aircraft carriers, missiles and every other major defense program in the arsenal. I was told when I was hired to create an auditable view of the data. There was a graveyard of contractors spanning decades that had failed to do this job who had come before me.

After reviewing the past costs and contract deliverables made by my predecessors who had been working on this problem for many years, it was clear no one assigned to work on the problem knew what they were doing. In later testimony, I would learn that many of the earlier contractors said they were operating under orders to not create auditable data. You have to understand.

In Washington D.C., the only purpose for a government technology contract is not to make deliveries. It is about billable hours and junk. It is about getting rich. Create problems and make a career out of getting paid not to solve them. Everyone scratching each other's backs, revolving doors, the Washington D.C. way.

To make a long story short, as a result of my unique technical approach we easily gained access to all the data we needed, and in a very short time I uncovered the diabolical reason why the Pentagon has never produced an audited financial statement.

`People steal, and they work together to cover it up.`

There are literally **hundreds of thousands of people** -robotic drones in and around the government today who break the law by turning a blind-eye to keep the riches they are receiving off the backs of taxpayers hidden from public scrutiny. These people will take any measure to stop being exposed. Out of all the senior executives that I have ever worked with in my lifetime, I have to say that the government attracts the most despicably evil collection of unskilled buffoons I have ever encountered. Everyone who has ever worked there knows deep down, for example, that an audit will show that the majority of the people who work in the Pentagon can be eliminated completely, but they never will. They control all that money. Can anyone remember the really expensive hammers? No audit, no visibility into expenditures that are bankrupting the country.

DEFENSE SPENDING (BILLIONS OF DOLLARS)

China

Saudi Arabia

India

France

Russia

United Kingdom

Germany

United States

The United States Spends More On Defense Than The Next Seven Countries Combined

To give you just a sniff of the arrogance at my former company, one of my co-workers was caught after three years billing a contract full time for himself and another person while he attended college full time working on a PhD. The other person was a research assistant he hired to be paid by the government, but work for him – helping him get his PhD. He didn't get caught until he graduated and left the contract and the billing went down. The money he was paid was never recouped. I could give thousands of examples like these that happen each day in our government and nobody cares. It is beyond out of control. It's just plain ridiculous that all this is still happening, and nobody cares.

Here's how it works. Defense contractors bill the government $200 per hour for the same services they provide other government agencies for half that amount, then they pay the people performing the work $50 per hour in salary and benefits. The rest goes directly into corporate profits that are redistributed to executives and board members in the form of stock and bonuses. I made a mountain of cash working at SAIC from 2004 until 2011, cashing in big time when the company held its IPO in 2006.

100

GENESIS -Manifesto

In response to my whistleblower complaint which contained substantial documented evidence of systemic crimes and malfeasance committed by SAIC for many years, the Department of Defense (DoD) Inspector General (IG) issued a ruling in my case that said, '**federal government contractors have no statutory protections from whistleblower retaliation under the law. Therefore Mr. Edwards does not qualify for any protection from retaliation after making his complaint.**'

```
John Stuart Edwards incurred over $130,000 in legal fees over
four years after fighting off continuous attacks from the
military industrial complex – and then Congress intervened on
his behalf, and the corrupt DoD IG Jon Rymer finally admitted
defeat. But then, Congress changed hands and turned a blind eye
while corrupt bureaucrats have continuously attacked John and
his family by dispatching federal agents to their home in order
to intimidate and threaten their lives.
```

Imagine it this way. You come home and discover someone is murdered in your driveway. You call the police and they tell you that it's not a crime because of the way they have decided to interpret the law that day. You say, "That is ridiculous, what if they come after me?" and the police officer says there is nothing she can do about it. That night, the murderer returns to the scene and kills you.

Now it doesn't matter what happened to you. You're dead. All you can do going forward is haunt their existence. I have chosen to do that by creating a permanent record of my experiences working for the corrupt U.S. federal government in order to inform future generations of humans. I have made arrangements to permanently archive and protect all my publications for future use and research, so if you are reading this in 1,000 years – lucky you.

My Manifesto ~by John Stuart Edwards

*My **Manifesto** was inspired by President Eisenhower's Farewell Address and President Kennedy's Inaugural Address in the **year** that I was born.*

VISION -Manifesto

The Future of Human Life

- *During the next half-century, disease prevention and cellular regeneration can transform health care and extend life.*
- *Community ecosystems in the United States can become environmentally secure.*
- *Wire-free transmission networks and receivers can provide ubiquitous electricity and communications anywhere around the globe.*
- *Nourishment technologies can transform molecules into potable water and revolutionize the production and portability of food and medicine.*
- *Problem solving can be unconstrained by biological intelligence that is supplemented with AI.*
- *Robotics can transform transportation, services and manufacturing economies.*
- *And the world can have peace.*

Around the globe, bold goals like these are being pursued by visionaries within the constraints of government paradigms, ignoring the fact that technology is every government's silver bullet.[5] At the present rate of technology disruption, a country or perhaps even a large corporation can now compete for total global dominance of people in the next century by erecting a digital throne built upon a sea of knowledge that is fueled by artificial super intelligence to rule the world.

PROBLEM -Manifesto in a nutshell

United States federal government-wide technology expenditures exceed $100 BILLION per year and will surpass $1 TRILLION total spending during the next decade.[6] There are more than 85,000 information technology civil servants feeding off the federal technology spending trough right now.[7]

The spending "cartel" is a revolving door arrangement between politicians, lobbyists, bureaucrats and contractors in Washington D.C. who control, distribute and consume billions of taxpayer dollars for power and personal gain.

Unfortunately for Americans, a fraud scheme that will bankrupt the country and potentially *destroy the Republic* is underway. It is being carried out by the U.S. federal government technology spending cartel under the protection of the military industrial complex. My whistleblower complaint against DoD halted the waste of over $600 Million in just one year on technology. That barely scratched the surface.

To put this in perspective, consider that in the current fiscal year, the United States will spend **many Trillion** more than it receives in taxes and increase the national debt to over **$27 Trillion in 2020.**

```
"U.S. Government spending at the federal level is out of control
and nobody cares. Who is steering this runaway train? The
politicians are all useless. The Donor Class? All the
billionaires in the world. Is humanity just an experiment in a
continuous game of thrones?"
```

Twenty years ago, in 1999, the nation's debt stood at $5.6 Trillion and the United States Treasury took in $128 Billion more in taxes than it spent that year for a budget surplus.[8]

My Manifesto extends the work that I started in my fight against widespread corruption in Washington D.C.

SOLUTION ONE -Manifesto

*There are **Five Simple Actions** that if taken together will break the **Cycle of Fraud** and create **Manifesto Savings** that can be used to achieve the **Manifesto Vision** and help prevent the nation from going bankrupt.*

My Manifesto will achieve the following outcomes:

- Save taxpayers $65 Billion
- Eliminate 58,000 federal government jobs
- Empower Whistleblowers to fearlessly report waste, fraud and abuse
- Consolidate all federal government technology investment portfolios to reduce costs
- Streamline administrative operations and assign accountability for results with visibility for taxpayers

Cut Spending:

Congress and the President must enact legislation beginning with the 2021 fiscal year budget to **cut all federal technology spending** 10 percent each year, for ten years. Savings for taxpayers will be over $65 Billion.[9]

Cut Bureaucrats:

Congress and the President must enact legislation beginning with the fiscal year 2021 budget to **cut federal government technology bureaucrats** by 25 percent per year, for four years to achieve a staffing level of 27,000 by 2025.[10]

Protect Whistleblowers

who report fraud, waste and abuse by enacting legislation that guarantees reimbursement of all legal expenses for anyone who makes a protected whistleblower complaint in accordance with the law.

Punish Whistleblower Retaliation

by enacting legislation that imposes mandatory prison sentences for anyone in government convicted of whistleblower retaliation. If the person is a government contractor, the law should permit the government to cancel the contract.

Consolidate Technology Investment Management:

Congress and the President must enact legislation beginning with the fiscal year 2021 budget to eliminate all department and agency level Chief Information Officers (CIO) except for the Department of Homeland Security (DHS), Department of Defense (DoD) and the DNI.[11] The DHS CIO will oversee all non-defense federal tech spending, the DoD CIO will oversee all defense tech spending and the DNI will oversee all intelligence tech spending.

In December 2011, after leaving SAIC, I published this technical "fun" video to explain in layman's terms precisely how the federal government can save $40 Billion in technology spending at the Department of Defense.[12]
After seeing this video, the Department of Homeland Security hired me to be the *Lead Modernization Architect* for the national E-Verify system. My job was to design and modernize that system for comprehensive immigration reform.

The current organization and management of information technology spending in the U.S. federal government is too costly and unsustainable. The U.S. is falling further behind other nations, especially China. This problem cannot be fixed by the people who feed from the taxpayer trough. Every single employee who works for the federal government today participates in the technology cartel either directly, or passively with their silence, and each employee profits from corruption in the form of lifetime pensions and benefits paid for by taxpayers. Unfortunately, most Americans are unaware of what occurs behind the scenes because they don't work for the government. It's so bad it is impossible to believe.

> Now think about that $65 Billion in Manifesto Savings... and saving the world from government tyranny that is fueled by greed to make the world a better place.

SOLUTION TWO -Manifesto

By taking six simple low-cost accountability steps together, the United States **Congress** can restore dignity & respect to a government that has so much corruption today. If our representatives don't act now, perhaps some future generation will read this and then they will know what to do, if we still have a country.

Confirm

nominees for the Merit Systems Protection Board (MSPB) and restore a quorum so that whistleblower cases may be heard.

Reform

the **Council of the Inspectors General on Integrity and Efficiency**—which oversees IGs at federal agencies by making it a crime to conceal lawlessness by its members.

Fix FOIA

by adding criminal penalties for violations of the **Freedom of Information Act** for government officials that illegally withhold information from the public or alter official records prior to release.

Vote for Term Limits

to end government corruption by calling an immediate vote for **Senate Joint Resolution 1** & **House Joint Resolution 20** to amend the **Constitution of the United States** to limit the number of terms that a Member of **Congress** may serve.

And add these actions already offered in Solution One -Manifesto

Protect

whistleblowers who report fraud, waste and abuse by enacting legislation that guarantees reimbursement of all legal expenses for anyone who makes a protected whistleblower complaint in accordance with the law.

Punish

whistleblower retaliation by enacting legislation that makes retaliation a crime and imposes mandatory prison sentences for anyone in government convicted of whistleblower retaliation.

My Manifesto is the instruction manual for reforming the management of a government that is spiraling wildly out of control and must be stopped before civilization is completely destroyed.

*John Stuart Edwards is a U.S. Department of Defense **Whistleblower** and retired Marine Corps Mustang who uncovered nearly **$1 Billion** in fraud by his* *employer, the powerful defense & intelligence contractor* **Science Applications International Corporation (SAIC).** *John was retaliated against by the company in May 2011, for blowing the whistle on executives and Board members who were caught stealing billions of dollars from taxpayers each year.*

During the months before John Stuart Edwards blew the whistle, he was named as one of **SAIC's top 100 employees** *throughout the company (SAIC had 41,000 employees nationwide) and received the* **Technology Development and Analysis Annual Achievement Award** *which is the highest honor that the company bestows for its technical employees on an annual basis. John was also appointed to be a* **Charter Member of SAIC's Technical Review Board** *for United States Homeland and Civilian Technology Solutions just one month before he blew the whistle on corruption, and then John Stuart Edwards was fired from the company in retaliation.*

NOTES

1. Read Exercise of Power: American Failures, Successes, and a New Path Forward in the Post-Cold War World by Robert Gates 2020.

2. Environmental security is the viability for life support and prevention or repair of damage to the environment.

3. Artificial intelligence – AI, sometimes called machine intelligence, is intelligence demonstrated by machines, in contrast to the natural intelligence displayed by humans and other animals.

4. Robotics includes the use of robots and computer systems for their control, sensory feedback, and information processing.

5. The term 'silver bullet' refers to an action which cuts through complexity and provides an immediate solution to a problem.

6. See the ITDashboard.gov and the Office of Management and Budget Analytical Perspectives websites. Includes estimated classified technology spending and the technology modernization fund.

7. Source: U.S. Office of Personnel Management FedScope Portal

8. Sources: See Budget deficit website, Historical debt website, Debt forecast website, and the Budget breakdown website.

9. Savings computed as $1 Trillion minus (2020-$10B + 2021-$9B + 2022-$8.1B + 2023-$7.29B + 2024-$6.561B + 2025-$5.905B + 2026-$5.315B + 2027-$4.784B + 2028-$4.305B + 2029-$3.875B) = $65.135B in total savings.

10. Personnel cuts computed as 85,000 minus (2020-21,250 + 2021-15,937 + 2022-11,953 + 2023-8,965) = 58,105 in total personnel cuts.

11. Director of National Intelligence

12. Contact me to discuss the details.

Deborah Jeffrey – Vice Chairperson – CIGIE

Deborah Jeffrey is the Vice Chairperson of the Integrity Committee for the Council of the Inspectors General on Integrity and Efficiency

Are you a **RED PILL** or **BLUE PILL** American?

If you are a **BLUE PILL** American, please stop reading now and go back to your life in the land of fake news where my constitutional rights are being trampled upon each day under your blind eye.

The two pills are metaphors for humans, not political parties. If you don't know what that means, take the **BLUE PILL.**

Through extensive experimentation for more than four decades, I have proven beyond a reasonable doubt that the root cause of all Fake News in the United States is Whistleblower Retaliation carried out by the **Council of Inspectors General on Integrity and Efficiency.**[1] If you don't know what that means, take the **BLUE PILL.**

I have submitted a **Petition to the Government for a Redress of Grievances** to all three branches of the U.S. government and every federal agency that contains **six simple legislative solutions** that if enacted right now, will end all fake news and whistleblower retaliation in the U.S. federal government immediately. It is the $E=mc^2$ to end government corruption. If you don't know what that means, take the **BLUE PILL.**

It is probable that only a small fraction of all the people in the entire world possess the intelligence & basic education to understand what all this means. No worries, the entire textbook is 'encoded' to be understood by a future super artificial intelligence and funded for the next 100 years to help future generations of humans survive. If you don't know what that means, take the **BLUE PILL.**

If obtaining quality **K**nowledge[2] about what is really happening inside the U.S. government is not real news to you, take the **BLUE PILL.**

So, if you think that you have the mind for it – you can take the **RED PILL** now simply by reading the *press inquiry* below and the website capitolhellway.com. The choice is yours. This is, after all, a college level textbook – and this lesson is called. *"A Simple Solution for Americans – The Silver Bullet to End All Government Corruption Right Now."* If you don't know what that means, take the **BLUE PILL.**

```
For anyone still reading, here is your RED PILL.
```

Read the remainder of this textbook... and please contact us if you have questions. Solving problems humans face is a serious issue for serious minds in this country that have the capacity for original thought and an imagination that believes in truth, justice and especially ***the rule of law.***

Press Inquiry – Capitol Hellway Media Company LLC – Naples Florida

From: Capitol Hellway Media Company
Mon, Dec 30, 2019 at 7:56 AM
   To: **Council of Inspectors General on Integrity and Efficiency**
   Reference: docket number DC-1221-16-0227-W-1

Good morning, My company has published direct testimonial and documentary evidence that proves beyond a reasonable doubt that the **Council of Inspectors General on Integrity and Efficiency** is illegally influencing the 2020 Presidential election by concealing lawlessness by its members to CONCEAL RACIAL DISCRIMINATION Against Eight African American Federal Government Workers.

   The necessary evidence backed up by recordings is posted at the following link for your reference.

   Also attached are two recent whistleblower complaints submitted using your procedures on 12/29/2019 for you to investigate, or continue to cover up.

   All the evidence, along with this textbook will be published next year by my company, and will all be submitted into evidence when my Whistle-blower case docket number DC-1221-16-0227-W-1 is finally heard; and I intend to prove at the highest court if necessary that I have been retaliated against for over four years (now) by your IG's at Labor, NLRB and DHS for reporting racial discrimination and that the damages and torture carried out by your organization's corruption has destroyed my family's entire life. It might be a year, four years, or 50. It is in my will for my grandchildren to have the means to fight after I am gone if we are killed by you. But you will be held accountable for the crimes you have committed against me one day. All of you will.

Would you care to comment for our textbook? Deadline is this Friday at noon so we can make our publishing deadlines. The DHS and NLRB Inspectors General are obviously collaborating in real time to alter documents to conceal death threats and constitutional rights violations carried out by DHS agents and SES NLRB staff within the last 90 days against me – a known journalist and, as the video with DHS agents on November 8, 2019 proves – a citizen who was considering a run for the U.S. Congress to represent Florida as an Independent in the 2020 election at the time.

You know. I know you are all deeply evil and corrupt narcissists fighting for your politician's goals. But those days are numbered now. The fact that your IGs are still violating the constitutional rights of American Citizens on behalf of a major political party to prevent public consideration of the six legislative acts that I proposed is the real tell of your arrogance.

    You all have blind eyes that you will not be permitted to hide
    anymore.

Only corrupt IG's would oppose all those proposals and all of you do. In all of your existence as IG's, you never came up with anything as simple and elegant and effective as the six? It would put you out of a job because all your faux investigations to retaliate against whistleblowers and of course all your political campaign work would have to come to an end.

But a new year is upon us. And change is on the horizon. By you, or by me or the next generation or the one after that. That is your choice. And you have to make it soon.

To send responses – reply to this email.

Disclaimer: This email and all responses will be published continuously for at least the next 100 years.

Happy New Year

John Stuart Edwards

Entrepreneur

Capitol Hellway Media Company LLC

Naples, Florida

2 Attachments

Whistleblower Complaint DHS December 29 2019.pdf

Whistleblower Complaint NLRB December 29 2019.pdf

THE FEBRUARY 5, 2020 RESPONSE FROM

 Integrity Committee
Council of the Inspectors General on Integrity and Efficiency
1717 H Street, NW, Suite 825, Washington, DC 20006 • Integrity-Complaint@cigie.gov

The IC thoroughly reviewed the allegations and supporting information provided and determined that it will take no further action on this matter at this time.

Deborah Jeffrey – Vice Chairperson – Integrity Committee – Council of the Inspectors General on Integrity and Efficiency[3]

The statutory mission of the Council of the Inspectors General (CIGIE) Integrity Committee (IC) is to receive, review and refer for investigation allegations of wrongdoing made against an Inspector General (IG). The failure by Deborah Jeffrey – Vice Chairperson – Integrity Committee – Council of the Inspectors General on Integrity and Efficiency to carry out this statutory mission is a violation of the law. Unfortunately, there is no punishment for breaking this law, so corruption has invaded the entire federal government.

MORE DIRECT EVIDENCE OF A COVER-UP by **Inspector General Scott Dahl**

FOIA REQUESTS THAT WILL BLOW THE LID OFF THE SECRET PROTECTION SOCIETY INSIDE THE U.S. GOVERNMENT

January 6 2020 Letter – NLRB Chairman to Council of the Inspectors General on Integrity and Efficiency

January 29 2020 Letter – NLRB Chairman to Council of the Inspectors General on Integrity and Efficiency

FOIA Number NLRB-2020-000480 for an evidentiary listing that proves additional crimes by the Council of the Inspectors General on Integrity and Efficiency and its members are being concealed.

and Whistleblower case docket number DC-1221-16-0227-W-1 which can be read here:

For her eager and active participation in concealing crimes by Inspectors General and turning a blind eye to government corruption, **Deborah Jeffrey** will be a featured corrupt bureaucrat in the new textbook in Part III, **"Case Studies on Federal Government Corruption, Malfeasance and Reform in the 21st Century"** to be published on Labor Day 2020.

Reform the Council of the Inspectors General on Integrity and Efficiency—which oversees IGs at federal agencies by making it a crime for Deborah Jeffrey and others to conceal lawlessness by its members. Deborah Jeffrey needs to be sent to prison for the damage she has done to this country by turning a blind eye to lawlessness by the Inspectors General and Systemic Racism at the U.S. Department of Labor.

The Edwards Dossier is a textbook that was engineered to create a platform for future generations of humans to <u>**"KILL"**</u> corrupt government bureaucrats and politicians who retaliate against Whistleblowers and destroy lives.[4]

NOTES

1. The Council of the Inspectors General on Integrity and Efficiency (CIGIE) is an independent entity established within the executive branch to address integrity, economy and effectiveness issues that transcend individual Government agencies and aid in the establishment of a professional, well-trained and highly skilled workforce in the Offices of Inspectors General.

2. **THE KNOWLEDGE EQUATION**

Knowledge equals the total sum of the thoughts and experiences between a question and its answer over time

3. **Jeanetta M. Lee** – Government Information Specialist for the CIGIE has acknowledged receipt of all the following Freedom of Information Act Requests.

—

On Tue, Feb 18, 2020 at 11:24 AM Capitol Hellway Media Company <capitolhellway @gmail.com> wrote:

ATTENTION: CIGIE FOIA Public Liaison, Deborah Waller, Supervisory Government Information Specialist; (202) 616-1210 or designated representative.

Date of Request: **2/18/2020**

Capitol Hellway Media Company LLC

Attachment- FOIA Request Tracking Number NLRB-2020-000503

The Capitol Hellway Media Company LLC is investigating alleged corruption in the US government by federal officials who represent your organization including but not limited to the current CIGIE Vice Chairperson of the Integrity Committee Deborah Jeffrey.

The purpose of this FOIA request is to obtain the records for complaints made to the Council of the Inspectors General on Integrity and Efficiency against any employee of the National Labor Relations Board or Department of Labor or Department of Homeland Security or Council of the Inspectors General on Integrity and Efficiency from **September 15, 2015 to February 18, 2020**.

The attachment is provided to assist with your search for records and aid with your recollection of some of the evidence you have received.

Please supply this information by responding to this email.

John Stuart Edwards

Entrepreneur

Capitol Hellway Media Company LLC

Naples, Florida

—

On Mon, Feb 17, 2020 at 9:12 AM Capitol Hellway Media Company <capitolhellway @gmail.com> wrote:

ATTENTION: CIGIE FOIA Public Liaison, **Deborah Waller**, Supervisory Government Information Specialist; (202) 616-1210 or designated representative.

Date of Request: **2/17/2020**

Capitol Hellway Media Company LLC

Reference: a) USDOJ/FBI FOIPA Request No.: 1344781-000 Subject: Meeting Minutes for the CIGIE Integrity Committee dated October 9, 2018 signed by **David M. Hardy** - Section Chief Record/Information Dissemination Section Information Management Division

The Capitol Hellway Media Company LLC is investigating alleged corruption in the US government by federal officials who represent your organization including but not limited to the current CIGIE **Chair Michael E. Horowitz** and CIGIE Vice-Chair Allison C. **Lerner**. This is a matter of urgent public concern.

The purpose of this FOIA request is to obtain and make available to the public:

1. a) All Integrity Committee Meeting Minute records for the period **April 16, 2018 to February 5, 2020 (IAW reference a)**.

2. b) The TOTAL NUMBER of Inspectors General involuntarily removed from federal employment by the Council of the Inspectors General on Integrity and Efficiency between **March 21, 1996** (Executive Order 12993) and **February 5, 2020**.

Please supply this information in accordance with the reference by responding to this email.

An image of Reference a) is attached to this email to assist with your response to this FOIA request.

John Stuart Edwards

Entrepreneur

Capitol Hellway Media Company LLC

Naples, Florida

—

On Thu, Feb 13, 2020 at 10:46 AM Capitol Hellway Media Company <capitolhellway@gmail.com> wrote:

ATTENTION: CIGIE FOIA Public Liaison, Deborah Waller, Supervisory Government Information Specialist; (202) 616-1210 or designated representative.

Date of Request: **2/13/2020**

Capitol Hellway Media Company LLC

The Capitol Hellway Media Company LLC is investigating corruption in the US government by federal officials who may have had contact with your organization. The purpose of this request is to obtain a listing of all communications during the period **April 16, 2018 to February 5, 2020** between current National Labor Relations Board Chairman John F. Ring or his representatives and any member or representative of the Council of the Inspectors General on Integrity and Efficiency.

The types of contacts to be included in this request are not limited to all common forms of communication such as official letters, emails, meetings, handwritten notes and phone conversations that took place on duty time. This request includes within its scope ALL communications, including private email accounts and social interactions involving any matter of interest to the NLRB and the Council of the Inspectors General on Integrity and Efficiency.

For this request, only the date and type of contact is requested, displayed as a list in this manner:

Date – Type of Contact (Letter, Email, Meeting, Notes, Phone Call, Other)

No other documentation related to these communications is requested, at this time. For example, for a letter sent to or received by the NLRB on a specific date could be displayed like this:

1/6/2020 – Letter

1/21/2020 – Letter

1/29/2020 – Letter

The authority to engage in investigative journalism and report malfeasance by government officials who violate the law is covered by the US Constitution and this request is protected under the Freedom of Information Act in order to inform the public. You may follow this developing story at this link and in the textbook Part III, **"Case Studies on Federal Government Corruption, Malfeasance and Reform in the 21st Century"** to be published on Labor Day 2020.

Have a nice day.

John Stuart Edwards

Entrepreneur

Capitol Hellway Media Company LLC

Naples, Florida

—

On Wed, Feb 12, 2020 at 5:38 PM Capitol Hellway Media Company <capitolhellway @gmail.com> wrote:

Deborah Jeffrey – Vice Chairperson – Integrity Committee – Council of the Inspectors General on Integrity and Efficiency

Ms. Jeffrey,

Thank you for acknowledging receipt of my request for additional information today.

On a related matter, I would like to be the first to congratulate you on being selected by my editors as a featured corrupt bureaucrat in my new textbook, *"Petition to the Government for a Redress of Grievances"* to be published on Labor Day.

Here is a link to the unedited crowd-sourced version of the book's 'Introduction' section that includes our communications with you that you can monitor if you want. Photos of you are starting to pour in. We are collaborating with other whistleblowers facing obstruction by your organization and expect blockbuster downloads for the free book at universities around the globe after roll-out on every possible platform and format known to us at this time, just in time for the election.

Introduction to Federal Government Corruption, Malfeasance and Reform

Meet Deborah Jeffrey – Vice Chairperson – Integrity Committee – Council of the Inspectors General on Integrity and Efficiency

If you would like to offer any additional feedback for the book along with your answers to the two questions below related to the complaint you are refusing to investigate, please contact me soon. Also, if you ever reverse your decision to not investigate the written death threats made by three of your members against me and my family let us know. Remember, there will be another edition of the book published every four years for the next 100 years – so there will be plenty of opportunities to update history about your conduct if it improves.

Behold. The day of reckoning is coming. There is still time to do the right thing, but like an hourglass your time is about to run out in ways you cannot see or comprehend.

Hope to hear from you soon, and congratulations again on being selected as one of my featured corrupt bureaucrats in the book. After hearing today what Whistleblower Darrell Whitman has to say about you and your members, you definitely deserve that designation.

John Stuart Edwards sends

—

On Wed, Feb 12, 2020 at 4:04 PM Integrity-Complaint <Integrity-Complaint @cigie.gov> wrote:

Dear Mr. Edwards,

We have received your emails and have forwarded your questions to the Integrity Committee for consideration.

Sincerely,

Integrity Committee Working Group

—

From: **Capitol Hellway Media Company** <capitolhellway @gmail.com>
Date: Tue, Feb 11, 2020 at 3:50 PM
Subject: Fwd: Press Inquiry – Capitol Hellway Media Company LLC – Naples Florida
To: <integrity-Complaint @cigie.gov>, <cigie.information @cigie.gov>
Cc: CapitolHellway <capitolhellway @gmail.com>, <yovi.alvarez @mail.house.gov>, <andrea.morales @mail.house.gov>
RE: Deborah Jeffrey letter dated Feb 5, 2020 – Complaint to the Integrity Committee (attached)

Dear Ms. Deborah Jeffrey – Vice Chairperson Integrity Committee,

Recent press reports by Politico and Bloomberg Law point to additional evidence that NLRB Inspector General David Berry has a very long history of abuse of power and racial discrimination that your organization is clearly covering up on his behalf.

I have two follow up questions to your Feb 5 letter which states, "The IC thoroughly reviewed the allegations and supporting information provided and determined, pursuant to Integrity Committee Policies and Procedures – 2018, paragraph 7 .C., that it will take no further action on this matter at this time."

The Integrity Committee Policies and Procedures – 2018, paragraph 7 .C. that you referenced provides six specific actions the IC is authorized to take, including referral to another agency such as the Department of Justice. You reference paragraph 7 .C. to support your determination, yet your letter mysteriously omits the specific action taken by you which suggests that your continued involvement is a conflict of interest. Any reasonable person would expect a more comprehensive response to such severe allegations including death threats, yet yours was dismissive and arrogant.

It will be fascinating for normal people in this country who don't live in the swamp to learn how a so-called "Integrity Committee" for Inspectors General will close an investigation of its members on such severe charges as violation of rights and racism and death threats without speaking with the two people who made the complaint. You reference nothing in your response that remotely suggests that this is not a massive cover-up of crimes committed by your members. You have confirmed the need for this legislation:

Reform the Council of the Inspectors General on Integrity and Efficiency—which oversees IGs at federal agencies by making it a crime to conceal lawlessness by its members.

Question 1: Which specific action listed in paragraph 7 .C. was the IC letter dated Feb 5 based on and what is the justification for that determination?

Hopefully, Congressman Mario Diaz-Balart will demand you answer this question – his staff is copied here.

Question 2: On what specific authority in Integrity Committee Policies and Procedures – 2018 was Mr. Dahl recused from this matter – why was he permitted to not participate?

Your "turn a blind eye" tactic has worked for your organization for many years and has destroyed this country, but that time is coming to an end, and you will be held accountable.

Behold. The day of reckoning is here – Labor Day 2020.

John Stuart Edwards

Entrepreneur

Capitol Hellway Media Company LLC
Naples, Florida
—

On Wed, Feb 5, 2020 at 11:06 AM Integrity-Complaint <Integrity-Complaint @cigie.gov> wrote:

Dear Mr. Edwards,

Please see the attached letter from the Integrity Committee.

Sincerely,

Integrity Committee Working Group

4. Use of a Metaphor to explain how it feels.

The Edwards Dossier

An Ode to the Whistle-Blow

*"I blew the Whistle on government corruption in September 2015, and have been retaliated against continuously ever since because the **U.S. Merit Systems Protection Board** (MSPB) lacks a quorum and, as my case will prove, the Whistleblower Laws in the United States are dangerous and irresponsible and a threat to all freedoms guaranteed by the Constitution. The entire system of checks and balances lacks accountability at every level in every branch of the U.S. federal government."* **John Stuart Edwards**

Introduction to Federal Government Corruption, Malfeasance and Reform

Meet **Deborah Jeffrey** – Vice Chairperson – Integrity Committee – Council of the Inspectors General on Integrity and Efficiency[1]

John Stuart Edwards v. U. S. Department of Labor
Docket Number DC-1221-16-0227-W-1

Proof that these Bureaucrats and many more need to be Punished for concealing systemic racism against eight African American federal employees at the Department of Labor.

Mario Diaz-Balart – Member of Congress (R-FL)
Rosemary Lahasky – Special Assistant to President Donald J. Trump
John F. Ring – Chair, National Labor Relations Board (NLRB)
Lauren McFerran - Board Member, NLRB
Peter B. Robb – NLRB General Counsel
David Berry – NLRB Inspector General
Prem Aburvasamy - NLRB Chief Information Officer
Chad Wolf – Acting Secretary of Homeland Security
Joseph V. Cuffari – DHS Inspector General
Aung Htein – Department of Labor Racist

MY TESTIMONY

"I swear before God that I personally witnessed eight highly competent African American federal employees be denied promotions and assignments that would enhance their careers. I was ordered to remain silent while a black woman was treated like a wild animal and herded into subservient jobs for many years because of the color of her skin."

U.S. DEPARTMENT OF LABOR
EMPLOYMENT AND TRAINING ADMINISTRATION

John Stuart Edwards
Deputy Director
Office of Information Systems & Techology

200 Constitution Avenue NW
Washington, DC 20210

Telephone: (202) 693-3816
BlackBerry: (202) 465-1511
E-mail: edwards.john.s@dol.gov

WE PRAY FOR HELP

John Stuart Edwards & Catherine Edwards

Naples, Florida

**CRIMES, COVERUPS & CONTINUOUS
WHISTLEBLOWER RETALIATION**

Read my **case** about **life threatening** violations of **5 U.S. Code §3331**, the oath of office, and other **high crimes & misdemeanors** still being committed today by current U.S. federal government workers and **corrupt career politicians** in Washington D.C. My case proves that senior officials in the U.S. government are ACTIVELY committing high crimes and misdemeanors including death threats to COVER UP RACISM against eight African Americans.[2]

ADOBE PDF

CLICK TO READ

CHARGES AGAINST CONGRESSMAN MARIO DIAZ-BALART

MULTIPLE VIOLATIONS OF

5 U.S. Code § 3331

the oath of office

&

WHISTLEBLOWER RETALIATION

CLICK TO READ

ADOBE PDF

CLICK TO READ

WHISTLEBLOWER COMPLAINT

DATED 12/29/2019

to the

U.S. DEPARTMENT OF HOMELAND SECURITY

CLICK TO READ

The Edwards Dossier is a textbook that was engineered to create a platform for future generations of humans to **"KILL"** corrupt government bureaucrats and politicians who retaliate against Whistleblowers and destroy lives.[3]

for

U.S. PRESIDENTIAL ELECTION YEARS

2020 – 2100

NOTES

1. **Hypocrisy** *defined*

Deborah Jeffrey has served as the Inspector General of the Corporation for National and Community Service since July 2012, following confirmation by the U.S. Senate. She has played an active role in the Inspector General community as a member of its Integrity Committee. Ms. Jeffrey spent most of her career in private practice as a partner in the law firm of Zuckerman Spaeder LLP, where she represented organizations and individuals in highstakes commercial and criminal litigation; defended senior government officials in high profile criminal, Inspector General and congressional investigations; and represented lawyers and law firms on matters of professional ethics, risk management and professional liability.

Appointed by the District of Columbia Court of Appeals as Vice Chair of the D.C. Board on Professional Responsibility, Ms. Jeffrey oversaw the attorney disciplinary system and enforced the Rules of Professional Conduct. She is the author of more than 30 opinions in disciplinary prosecutions.

Ms. Jeffrey began her legal career as a law clerk to the Honorable Harrison L. Winter, Chief Judge of the U.S. Court of Appeals for the Fourth Circuit. She holds a B.A. in Political Science from Johns Hopkins University and a J.D. from Harvard Law School, where she was Editor in Chief of the Harvard Civil Rights-Civil Liberties Law Review.

2.SENT ON 12/21/2019 to SENATOR RICK SCOTT, FLORIDA

VIA: Contact Senator Rick Scott website

Senator Scott,

First, my entire family wishes yours a blessed holiday season. My wife and I retired to Florida the week of Irma to start the second half of our lives together and have been terrorized by Congressman Mario Diaz-Balart for pursuing our American Dream of writing and art within months of our arrival. Since December 2017, Congressman Mario Diaz-Balart has been relentless in his terrorist conduct, so our holiday again this season is filled with stress and anxiety about whether we will be killed by this government and nobody cares. At this point your staff probably is discarding this communication to you so you never see it.

JUST IN CASE IT ESCAPES YOUR STAFF, THIS IS WHAT HAP-PENS WHEN WE GO OVER THREE YEARS WITHOUT THE SEN-ATE APPROVING THE MSPB NOMINEES

I PROPOSED THE FOLLOWING ACTIONS TO YOU IN SEPTEM-BER 2019, AND YOU IGNORED ME SENATOR. SINCE THEN, WE HAVE RECEIVED DEATH THREATS AND HAD AGENTS ATTACK OUR HOME. WE ARE UNSAFE AND NOBODY IN OUR GOVERN-MENT CARES BECAUSE I AM A WHISTLEBLOWER!

READ LETTER TO CONGRESS "I AM A WHISTLEBLOWER"

dated September 29, 2019

We have no expectation that you will lift a finger to protect us PROBABLY because we are not big contributors to your campaign. I am a no party affiliated Independent and my wife is a true Republican and we both love the President. But the swamp that surrounds him is the same swamp attacking us and our politicians don't care = so that should tell you something. Our freedom is completely gone, and none of our Republican politician's care. And one, Congressman Balart, is protected by the media down here because of his family – and so what's left for a citizen to do?

Anyway, here is the story below (tip of the iceberg) so you have it official through this odd communication channel – we will publish this notification to your office in the textbook. For the first edition next year, it is not an indictment by you. It is just another illustration of the unresponsiveness of all elected officials like you who go to Washington and forget who elected you. The people who need your help the most that you ignore after you go to Washington, just like everybody else.

Merry Christmas,

Read the evidence here:

THE EDWARDS DOSSIER

–

SENT ON 12/21/2019 to THE WHITE HOUSE

VIA: Contact the White House website

Can someone at the White please intervene now, if not for anything but to protect my family's life?

Probably not. Anyway, Merry Christmas.

–

SENT ON 12/21/2019 TO NATIONAL LABOR RELATIONS BOARD INSPECTOR GENERAL HOTLINE & DEPARTMENT OF HOME-LAND SECURITY INSPECTOR GENERAL HOTLINE & SENATOR RICK SCOTT – FLORIDA

VIA: for NLRB and SENATOR RICK SCOTT

Reference: NLRB December 16, 2019, response to **FOIA Case No. NLRB-2020-000161** & multiple reports about **Death Threats** made by

Synta Keeling in October 2019, and attacks by DHS agents in December 2017 & November 2019, reported by this company to all your offices many times.

The Capitol Hellway Media Company LLC received via regular U.S. mail ANOTHER very threatening letter TODAY from the **NLRB FOIA OFFICER SYNTA KEELING** (December 21, 2019).

The reason this letter is threatening is because it was received less than three months after her written death threats, six weeks after the last DHS agents assault, AND the letter signed by Synta Keeling just five days ago and received today is further direct evidence that the NLRB Inspector General's office and many others, including every NLRB field office and all IT system administrators including **Prem Aburvasamy** and **Eric Marks** and some of their subordinates are either intentionally destroying records; or the presence of the two records requested is being falsely reported by Keeling in order to cause further harm and suffering and damages to this company and its employees.

WHISTLEBLOWER RETALIATION NEEDS TO BE FEDERAL CRIME

FACT 1: Not only did the NLRB, DHS, Inspectors General and members of Congress and federal, state and local law enforcement officials and the public all receive the two records requested in **FOIA Case No. NLRB-2020-000161** on November 15, 2019, including the NLRB's Mr. Edwin Egee, Chairman, Executive Secretary and GC, and many others at the NLRB via multiple channels (email, online, fax, etc.) with electronic verification despite being BLOCKED by the NLRB CIO technology office, **Congressman Mario Diaz-Balart confirmed receipt of both documents and he needs to be held accountable as well.**

And the most clear and indisputable evidence that this is another THREAT is FACT 2 & 3:

FACT 2: The two Press Inquiries that Keeling denies there being a record of in **FOIA Case No. NLRB-2020-000161** were **INCLUDED INSIDE THE FOIA REQUEST submitted on FOIA online**, and according to Synta Keeling's letter we received today – we were too late. Keeling obviously thinks that she destroyed them and won't get caught when she wrote, "A search inquiry was made for the records sought. That search yielded no records responsive to your FOIA request." Again for the really low IQ folks in our government, the records were in the FOIA request asking for them to protect them from being destroyed. The records were received by everyone.

FACT 3: Synta Keeling is still employed.

Nevertheless, the following legislative reforms, if signed into law, will finally put an end to the continuous Whistleblower Retaliation that you have permitted or carried out, and help U.S. voters "KILL" all corruption in the U.S. federal government with six swift legislative acts:

Confirm nominees for the Merit Systems Protection Board (MSPB) and restore a quorum.

Protect whistleblowers who report fraud, waste and abuse by enacting legislation that guarantees reimbursement of all legal expenses for anyone who makes a protected whistleblower complaint in accordance with the law.

Punish whistleblower retaliation by enacting legislation that makes retaliation a crime and imposes mandatory prison sentences for anyone in government convicted of whistleblower retaliation.

Reform the Council of the Inspectors General on Integrity and Efficiency—which oversees IGs at federal agencies by making it a crime to conceal lawlessness by its members.

Fix FOIA by adding criminal penalties for violations of the Freedom of Information Act for government officials that illegally withhold information from the public or alter official records prior to release.

Vote for Term Limits to end government corruption by calling an immediate vote for Senate Joint Resolution 1 & House Joint Resolution 20 to amend the Constitution of the United States to limit the number of terms that a Member of Congress may serve.

But we all know you won't hear any of this from us. We are not big donors. And you are too damn busy protecting your own asses because you are all Whistleblower Retaliators and you are all corrupt!

Maybe next year you'll be held accountable, or maybe the next, or five years, or decade or sometime long after that. As long as we have life you know we will not quit, we will not stop. And that is your motive for wanting us dead. All the evidence we have presented proves that fact too.

To obtain the evidence, read this website and the textbook being published containing this report to you in 2020, and then again every four years thereafter until the end of time.

John & Cathy Edwards
Journalist & Pet Artist
Naples, Florida
3. Use of a Metaphor to explain how it feels.

Killing NLRB Chairman John Ring

President Trump's NLRB Chairman is a Criminal [1] [2]

John Stuart Edwards v. U. S. Department of Labor
Docket Number DC-1221-16-0227-W-1

Contains Complaints that these NLRB Bureaucrats are Criminals

John F. Ring – NLRB Chairman
Lauren McFerran - Board Member
Peter B. Robb – NLRB General Counsel
David Berry – NLRB Inspector General
Roxanne Rothschild – NLRB Executive Secretary
Elizabeth Bach – NLRB Special Counsel
Synta Keeling – NLRB FOIA Officer
Prem Aburvasamy – NLRB Chief Information Officer
Eric Marks – NLRB Deputy CIO
Hari Sharma – NLRB CIO Office
Ying Xing – NLRB CIO Office
Sivaram Ghorakavi – NLRB CIO Office

NLRB Chairman John F. Ring's corruption cartel committed high crimes and misdemeanors against two American citizens – a Journalist & Pet Artist – to COVER UP RACISM against eight African Americans.

HIGH CRIMES & MISDEMEANORS

These Two FOIA Requests along with the contents of *this article* contain access to all the direct evidence needed for law-abiding prosecutors to charge Chairman Ring & his entire staff with systemic racism, corruption, death threats & violation of Rights.[3]

read NLRB-2020-000275 – "ALL RECIPIENTS OF THIS 'REQUEST FOR INFORMATION' ARE ADVISED TO CONTACT LAW ENFORCEMENT OFFICIALS IMMEDIATELY UPON READING THIS 'REQUEST FOR INFORMATION' TO REPORT THAT YOU HAVE RECEIVED FACTUAL EVIDENCE ABOUT A THREAT OF VIOLENCE MADE AGAINST TWO AMERICAN CITIZENS IN NAPLES FLORIDA BY SENIOR U.S. GOVERNMENT OFFICIALS WHO STILL REMAIN CAPABLE OF KILLING THE COUPLE USING TAXPAYER FUNDED RESOURCES RIGHT NOW."

read NLRB-2020-000278 – "THIS FOIA REQUEST IS BELIEVED TO CONTAIN DIRECT EVIDENCE OF THE MOTIVE, MEANS AND OPPORTUNITY FOR TWELVE (12) CURRENT NATIONAL LABOR RELATIONS BOARD EMPLOYEES TO COMMIT HIGH CRIMES AND MISDEMEANORS THAT INCLUDE DEATH THREATS AND MULTIPLE SEVERE VIOLATIONS OF THE LAW."

ADOBE PDF
CLICK TO READ

WHISTLEBLOWER

COMPLAINT

DATED 12/29/2019

to the

NATIONAL LABOR RELATIONS BOARD (NLRB)

ADOBE PDF
CLICK TO READ

THE CHARGES

Systemic Racism, Corruption, Death Threats & Violation of Rights

WHISTLEBLOWER COMPLAINT

The first attack happened on December 6, 2017. The second attack in October 2019 in the form of death threat letters, and finally the third attack on November 8, 2019 against this company, a journalist and his pet artist wife in Naples Florida.

CLICK TO READ

In October 2019, Chairman Ring ordered two additional attacks including a threat of violence against a journalist and his wife and their company in Florida. First, Chairman Ring ordered his staff to issue two written death threats by U.S. mail to the couple and their small businesses. Then, a few weeks later, on November 8, 2019, after learning about the complaints from the Edwards' about the death threats they received, Chairman Ring issued direct orders to the Secretary of Homeland Security to use federal agents to retaliate against the couple for reporting the death threats to Congressman Mario Diaz-Balart (R-FL) and the FBI. The couple, a journalist and pet artist had just returned from the hospital after her kidney surgery when the agents trespassed without an appointment or any prior warning. The agents stated purpose on video was that they were following direct orders from the NLRB to intimidate both company employees and stop the couple and their businesses from publishing a textbook in 2020 that contains very detailed evidence and descriptions of Chairman Ring's crimes while serving as President Trump's chairman at the NLRB. Chairman Ring has violated the Constitution and every norm of a civil society. Chairman John F. Ring should not be supervising U.S. Labor Law. He should be in prison performing hard labor for the crimes he committed against this country and the Capitol Hellway Media Company LLC, a free media company in Naples Florida

DHS AGENTS CAUGHT ON VIDEO VIOLATING THE FIRST AMENDMENT RIGHTS OF NAPLES FLORIDA JOURNALIST

We are here on orders from NLRB Attorney Elizabeth Bach to violate your constitutional rights & discourage you from publishing your book.

12:00 PM
Friday, November 8, 2019
Veteran's Day Holiday Weekend
Capitol Hellway Media Company LLC

POLICE
DHS

PRESS INQUIRY

November 15, 2019

Mr. Egee,

We kindly offer you the opportunity to provide the Capitol Hellway Media Company LLC with a written response by email to the following press inquiry by Thanksgiving (deadline). This inquiry is sent by fax because, as you know, the NLRB CIO Prem Aburvasamy and Eric Marks are using taxpayer funding to obstruct all investigations into corruption at your agency, and your Inspector General David Berry is altering official government records in real time.

Question 1: What disciplinary actions is Chairman John F. Ring taking to punish NLRB FOIA Officer Synta Keeling? In October, Synta Keeling sent two letters on NLRB letterhead through the U.S. mail to a Naples, Florida journalist and this company to explicitly threaten his life and threaten litigation against this company for exposing widespread corruption and malfeasance at the NLRB during the Chairman's tenure.

Question 2: What is Chairman John F. Ring's relationship with his Executive Secretary Roxanne Rothschild?

Read related article here

Question 3: What disciplinary actions is Chairman John F. Ring taking to punish NLRB attorney Elizabeth Bach's blatant criminal acts to violate a Naples, Florida journalists' constitutional rights on November 8, 2019 [and December 6, 2017]?

Question 4: Is Chairman John F. Ring being blackmailed by any of these women or others?

Question 5: Mr. Egee, have you been asked to commit a high crime or misdemeanor in response to this press inquiry?

141

FIRST PRESS INQUIRY >

Edwin Egee
OFFICE OF CONGRESSIONAL AND PUBLIC AFFAIRS
NATIONAL LABOR RELATIONS BOARD
WASHINGTON D.C.
202-208-3013

CLICK TO READ

November 13, 2019

We kindly offer you the opportunity to provide the **Capitol Hellway Media Company LLC** with a written response by email to capitolhellway@gmail.com to the following by Thanksgiving (deadline):

Capitol Hellway has obtained a copy of a whistleblower complaint submitted to the DHS Inspector General with the following complaint:

Oh yeah, it gets much worse for Chairman Ring and his wingman, the current NLRB General Counsel Peter B. Robb who was appointed by President Trump. Peter Robb took his first swing at this company within days after he was appointed in 2017.

THIS IS NOT THE FIRST TIME

On December 6, 2017 - a DHS agent and Collier County Sheriff's counterintelligence officer showed up at 9 a.m. on the doorstep of our journalists' residence in southwest Florida without any warning – not even a phone call – and coincidentally just six days after he first published his personal story about corruption at the NLRB.

CLICK TO READ

December 6, 2017 – THE FIRST NLRB ATTACK AGAINST THIS COMPANY & EMPLOYEES

The first attack happened on December 6, 2017. The second attack in October 2019 in the form of death threat letters, and finally the third attack on November 8, 2019 against this company, a journalist and his pet artist wife in Naples Florida.

THE NATIONAL LABOR RELATIONS BOARD

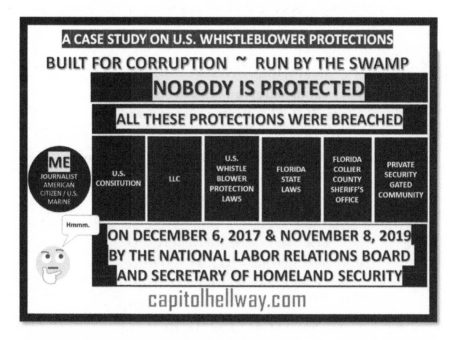

NLRB Chairman John F. Ring & General Counsel Peter B. Robb have Violated Every Law Under the Sun To Retaliate Against a Whistleblower Not Once, Not Twice, But Three Times in Two Years and the Entire Federal Government Won't Do A Damn Thing About It!

AMERICAN CITIZENS NEED A REMEDY FOR THESE ACTS OF TYRANNY BY NLRB Chairman John F. Ring AND HERE IT IS:

CALL CONGRESS

DEMAND RETROACTIVE CAPITAL PUNISHMENT FOR WHISTLEBLOWER RETALIATION AND PUNISH JOHN RING's ENTIRE CORRUPTION CARTEL FOR THEIR CRIMES AGAINST THE UNITED STATES OF AMERICA

If Whistleblower Retaliation was a Capital Crime then all these current NLRB employees could be on death row awaiting execution right now.[4]

John F. Ring – NLRB Chairman
Lauren McFerran - Board Member
Peter B. Robb – NLRB General Counsel
David Berry – NLRB Inspector General
Roxanne Rothschild – NLRB Executive Secretary
Elizabeth Bach – NLRB Special Counsel
Synta Keeling – NLRB FOIA Officer
Prem Aburvasamy – NLRB Chief Information Officer
Eric Marks – NLRB Deputy CIO
Hari Sharma – NLRB CIO Office
Ying Xing – NLRB CIO Office
Sivaram Ghorakavi – NLRB CIO Office
WE SAY LEGALLY KILL THEM ALL!

SUPPORT CAPITAL PUNISHMENT FOR WHISTLEBLOWER RETALIATION
Send NLRB Chairman John F. Ring to Hell

and the next experiment has already begun! stay tuned!

[**DISCLAIMER:** for the many thousands of very low IQ government attorneys funded by taxpayers who have been ordered to find another angle to attack this company and its employees again because you cannot comprehend what just happened to you, go ahead. The answers are all around you. The United States Marine Corps calls that B.O.H.I.C.A. – and Einstein called it the definition of insanity. Break the law, cover it up. Break the law, cover it up. Break the law, cover it up. This cycle is endless for bureaucrats in the D.C. Swamp and they have been conditioned for decades to respond no other way. No matter. The Capitol Hellway Media Company LLC has a 1,000 year vision. The U.S. Constitution and the sacrifices of all Wars inspires us to teach freedom loving people around the world the lengths a tyrannical government through a swamp-filled bureaucracy will go to stifle the First Amendment. This is why we have the Second Amendment and the rest of the Bill of Rights. To help citizens "kill" tyranny. "The Edwards Dossier" is an instruction manual to help Patriots learn how "kill" corruption using weapons of mass destruction at EVERY GOVERNMENT AGENCY IN THE WORLD. Our mission is to "kill" anyone whose entire life has been dedicated to committing corruption, retaliation and deceit. We believe that freedom of expression is more dangerous to governments than a nuclear bomb when used properly. Our mission is to "kill" every single corrupt motherfucker in the D.C. Swamp who violates the law, and we will never quit until the mission is completed!]

Contact Capitol Hellway Media Company LLC
tell us who you believe should die
COMING IN 2020
AND A VERY BIG FUCK YOU
TO ERIC MARKS!
read the evidence – this piece of shit can be fired today

AMERICANS HAVE A RIGHT TO KNOW

capitolhellway@gmail.com to contribute

NOTES

1. *"THE ACCUSED"*
John F. Ring – NLRB Chairman
Lauren McFerran - Board Member
Peter B. Robb – NLRB General Counsel
David Berry – NLRB Inspector General
Roxanne Rothschild – NLRB Executive Secretary
Elizabeth Bach – NLRB Special Counsel
Synta Keeling – NLRB FOIA Officer
Prem Aburvasamy – NLRB Chief Information Officer
Eric Marks – NLRB Deputy CIO
Hari Sharma – NLRB CIO Office
Ying Xing – NLRB CIO Office
Sivaram Ghorakavi – NLRB CIO Office

2. **Two FOIA requests provide readers with all the direct evidence needed for the U.S. government to fire & prosecute the TWELVE (12) CURRENT NATIONAL LABOR RELATIONS BOARD EMPLOYEES listed in footnote 1.**

read **NLRB-2020-000275** – "ALL RECIPIENTS OF THIS 'REQUEST

FOR INFORMATION' ARE ADVISED TO CONTACT LAW ENFORCE-
MENT OFFICIALS IMMEDIATELY UPON READING THIS 'REQUEST
FOR INFORMATION' TO REPORT THAT YOU HAVE RECEIVED FAC-
TUAL EVIDENCE ABOUT A THREAT OF VIOLENCE MADE AGAINST
TWO AMERICAN CITIZENS IN NAPLES FLORIDA BY SENIOR U.S.
GOVERNMENT OFFICIALS WHO STILL REMAIN CAPABLE OF
KILLING THE COUPLE USING TAXPAYER FUNDED RESOURCES
RIGHT NOW."

read **NLRB-2020-000278** – "THIS FOIA REQUEST IS BELIEVED
TO CONTAIN DIRECT EVIDENCE OF THE MOTIVE, MEANS AND
OPPORTUNITY FOR TWELVE (12) CURRENT NATIONAL LABOR
RELATIONS BOARD EMPLOYEES TO COMMIT HIGH CRIMES AND
MISDEMEANORS THAT INCLUDE DEATH THREATS AND MULTI-
PLE SEVERE VIOLATIONS OF THE LAW."

3. In a letter received on 1/6/2020 in the U.S. Mail, NLRB Counsel to the
Inspector General **James E. Tatum, Jr** wrote that a third FOIA Number
NLRB-OIG-2020-000285 had been assigned to the case.

Consequently, the two simple FOIA requests in footnote 2 will receive
three 'non' responses. **NLRB-2020-000275, NLRB-2020-000278** and
NLRB-OIG-2020-000285.

NOTE FOR ALL READERS: All the documents that the NLRB won't
provide by FOIA – including the "OIG-I-530 Report Dated January 3, 2017,"
will be published without redaction on Labor Day September 7, 2020.

2020 COURSE SYLLABUS

4. A capital crime is a crime that carries the possibility of a death sentence.

Death Threats by Synta Keeling at the NLRB

John Stuart Edwards and his wife, pet artist Cathy Edwards, received a series of **death threats** sent through the United States Postal Service within weeks of **Congressman Mario Diaz-Balart** (R-FL) confirming receipt of the entire online version of this textbook.

The death threats were issued in official letters signed by **Synta Keeling** and approved by her boss, **National Labor Relations Board** (NLRB) Chairman **John F. Ring** who was appointed by President Donald J. Trump.

Prior to his appointment to the NLRB, Mr. Ring served as a partner with the law firm Morgan Lewis. Ring has represented large corporation interests in collective bargaining, employee benefits, litigation, counseling, and litigation avoidance strategies. He has an extensive background violating collective bargaining agreements, most notably in the context of workforce restructuring and multi employer bargaining. Mr. Ring received his J.D. and B.A. from Catholic University of America.

The death threat letters from **Synta Keeling** stated that Mr. Edwards should "reasonably expect" violence to happen soon and threatened litigation to shut down his company, *Capitol Hellway Media Company LLC*, if this textbook is published. Synta Keeling is a highly partisan corrupt career government bureaucrat in Washington D.C. that enjoys the full protection of the NLRB despite committing multiple violations of the law for many years.

In response to a Freedom of Information Act request from John Stuart Edwards, Synta Keeling said, "the release of the requested information places individuals under a reasonable expectation of endangerment or threats, ongoing harassment," and went on to say that if Mr. Edwards continues to pursue this matter, his life is "reasonably at risk of being harmed."

John Stuart Edwards is a private citizen and the journalist who previously reported that **Synta Keeling** allegedly committed multiple crimes under the *Freedom of Information Act* and criminally concealed or altered official government records sent by the agency to the **National Archives and Records Administration** in 2016, 2017, 2018, and 2019, in order to conceal crimes committed by NLRB Chief Information Officer **Prem Aburvasamy,** his deputy **Eric Marks,** employees **Ying Xing, Hari Sharma, Sivaram Ghorakavi,** attorney **Elizabeth Bach,** Executive Secretary **Roxanne Rothschild** and Inspector General **David Berry.** The original whistleblower complaint was sent by email to the entire NLRB board on November 30, 2016. Synta Keeling is the NLRB's *Freedom of Information Act* (FOIA) officer.

From: Edwards, John
Sent: Wednesday, November 30, 2016 9:03 AM
To: Pearce, Mark G. <Mark.Pearce@nlrb.gov>; Miscimarra, Philip A. <Philip.Miscimarra@nlrb.gov>;
McFerran, Lauren <Lauren.McFerran@nlrb.gov>; Griffin, Richard F. <Richard.Griffin@nlrb.gov>

Subject: Request for Help

Good morning. My apologies for the intrusion but I have nowhere else to turn. I am your ACIO for
Mission Systems which includes NxGen, JCMS and FTS, along with all your scanners and the reporting
data warehouse. I joined the NLRB in April 2016 and have quietly done my very best to analyze, stabilize
and improve your systems at a lower cost and have produced significant results in a very short time. I
supervise 5 bargaining unit employees, and 4 GS14's along with about 10-12 contractors at this time and
have made great strides to improving both productivity and morale.

There is a very severe management issue that is spiraling out of control in the OCIO that I feel requires
very senior leadership intervention to resolve to protect the reputation of the NLRB and everyone
involved. I respectfully request your assistance in resolving the matter internally and appropriately.

I think the attached communications explain the current situation well, which is deteriorating quickly
into a hostile work environment for me and making me ill. I beg you to please ask my supervisor Eric
Marks and the OCIO Prem Aburvasamy to halt their active retaliation of me until a proper independent
investigation into the totality and validity of all the complaints involved can be done.

Synta Keeling's threats of 'harassment and violence' against the Edwards family were immediately reported to the FBI, the NLRB Inspector General and other senior government officials including Florida Senators Rick Scott, Marco Rubio and President Trump.

In response to the FBI complaint, NLRB attorney **Elizabeth Bach** dispatched federal agents to southwest Florida, on two occasions in violation of the law to threaten and intimidate Mr. Edwards and his family at their home. The agents covertly entered private property and made verbal threats to thwart the publication of this textbook.

Fix FOIA by adding criminal penalties for violations of the Freedom of Information Act for government officials that illegally withhold information from the public or alter official records prior to release.

FIRE SYNTA KEELING!

EVIDENCE

NLRB Death Threat Letter dated September 30, 2019 to Whistleblower John Stuart Edwards

NLRB Death & Litigation Threat Letter dated October 1, 2019 to Capitol Hellway Media Company LLC

"The Edwards Dossier" - Petition to the Government for a Redress of Grievances, 2020

Letter To Congress About Roxanne Rothschild

"HOW IS IT LEGAL FOR A GOVERNMENT LAWYER TO CONDUCT HERSELF THIS WAY?"
BREAKING NEWS IN THIS CASE

*Bloomberg Law reported that U.S. National Labor Relations Board **Chairman John Ring** filed a formal complaint against his **Inspector General David Berry** to have him fired for concealing evidence against **Roxanne Rothschild** and her husband **Bryan Burnett** and for ruthlessly retaliating against the whistleblower who blew the lid off their illegal operation. As of publication, there is no word yet whether there will be any arrests in the case before or after Rothschild and her husband are terminated. Roxanne Rothschild's husband is **Bryan Burnett - Chief Information Officer at Equal Employment Opportunity Commission**. You can only imagine the corrupt mess he has created over there after leaving the NLRB.*

Letter To Congress About Roxanne Rothschild

I am writing to you today to request that you Fire Roxanne Rothschild!

Roxanne Rothschild was promoted last week by the Trump administration despite being a lifetime federal government bureaucrat in Washington, D.C. who was **accused of leading a multi-year scheme with her husband to defraud the government of millions of dollars and retaliate against a whistleblower.** In an internal email dated October 22, 2018, the NLRB announced that effective immediately **Roxanne Rothschild** had replaced Gary Shinners as the Executive Secretary at **National Labor Relations Board** (NLRB).

Rothschild has a checkered past. The **NLRB Inspector General David Berry** received two whistleblower complaints about Ms. Rothschild in 2016 and 2017, that he has covered up. The complaints each contained substantial evidence that proves beyond a reasonable doubt that Ms. Rothschild participated in a scheme with her husband to commit contract fraud at the NLRB. The value of the fraud is millions of dollars. The complaints also show that Rothschild conspired with NLRB Chief Information Officer **Prem Aburvasamy** and his sidekick **Eric Marks** who worked for her husband to retaliate against a whistleblower who made a formal complaint to the Inspector General about the fraud.[1]

Senior Congressional Aid **Yovi Alvarez** who works for **Congressman Mario Diaz-Balart (R-FL)** can verify that the congressman was first made aware of this complaint on December 8, 2017, when **a federal agent from Homeland Security ambushed the home of a reporter in Florida** and **issued physical threats against his family** for speaking out about corruption at the NLRB.

A source close to Rothschild said, "Roxanne has nurtured some very special relationships with executives and board members and others who travel to D.C. each week from other states, far away from their loving wives and families."

According to another source, Rothschild has used her special personal relationships inside the office for her personal career advancement. Coincidentally, Ms. Rothschild met and married her current husband Bryan Burnett while working late nights together at the NLRB, based on eyewitness testimony. According to the NLRB Inspector General David Berry, **Bryan Burnett** left the agency sheepishly in early 2016, after a conflict of interest charge was first reported through the IG's hotline. The hotline is widely known at the agency to be a faux anonymous online system that was taken down earlier this year to shield the public from the massive corruption at the NLRB.[2]

The complaint says that **Roxanne Rothschild** and her husband **Bryan Burnett** together were in charge of the NLRB's technology investment portfolio for ten years from 2006 through December 2015. The couple managed a $160 million taxpayer funded budget for technology during that period, a sum that is more than 3x-times the cost of comparable government agencies to procure and administer technology for their employees. The NLRB has less than 1600 employees.

```
To put this in perspective, imagine that you were given $10,000
from taxpayers for each employee in your business to buy them a
new smart phone and laptop and keep them connected to the
Internet. Now imagine that you receive this amazing 'gift' of
```

```
$10,000 every single year you are in business. At the NLRB, they
did not use this money to buy anything new — and all the old
equipment and software was falling apart, so what happened to
all that money? There has been no investigation by the Inspector
General or any accountability for anyone and whenever it gets
reported, the whistleblower gets fired. That is the culture at
the NLRB. It is a deeply corrupt and evil organization.
```

The NLRB is an independent U.S. federal government agency with responsibilities for enforcing U.S. labor law. I was hired in April 2016, as Associate
CIO to fix a portfolio of failing software applications that suffered for many
years because of the incompetent management and corrupt practices of
Roxanne Rothschild and her husband **Bryan Burnett**. I was fired for
reporting their crimes.

> With this promotion, **Roxanne Rothschild** and **Bryan Burnett**
> together will rake in over $400,000 each year from taxpayers with
> a very comfortable retirement plan thanks to U.S. taxpayers and
> all the **Corruption at the National Labor Relations Board**.

Tell President Trump to end this insanity and "**Fire Roxanne Rothschild!**"
The time has come to require honesty and integrity from federal workers
at the NLRB.

Sent to:
U.S. SENATE
U.S. Senator Bill Nelson (D)
U.S. Senator Marco Rubio (R)
Florida Governor Rick Scott (R) – candidate
U.S. HOUSE OF REPRESENTATIVES – Florida 25th District
Congressman Mario Diaz-Balart (R)
Mary Barzee Flores (D) – candidate

NOTES

1. See U.S. Merit Systems Protection Board docket number DC-0752-17-0467-I-1 / John S. Edwards v. National Labor Relations Board / for case documents and material evidence filed on April 25, 2017, to substantiate all allegations against named individuals in this article.

2. See the article, "Punishing Corruption at the NLRB" for more details about this scumbag Inspector General.

Killing Eric Marks at the NLRB

Federal Deputy Chief Information Officer Eric Marks swindled more than $2 million from U.S. taxpayers.

Two FOIA requests provide readers with all the direct evidence needed for the U.S. government to fire & prosecute TWELVE (12) CURRENT NATIONAL LABOR RELATIONS BOARD EMPLOYEES, including Eric Marks.

read *NLRB-2020-000275* – *"ALL RECIPIENTS OF THIS 'REQUEST FOR INFORMATION' ARE ADVISED TO CONTACT LAW ENFORCEMENT OFFICIALS IMMEDIATELY UPON READING THIS 'REQUEST FOR INFORMATION' TO REPORT THAT YOU HAVE RECEIVED FACTUAL EVIDENCE ABOUT A THREAT OF VIOLENCE MADE AGAINST TWO AMERICAN CITIZENS IN NAPLES FLORIDA BY SENIOR U.S. GOVERNMENT OFFICIALS WHO STILL REMAIN CAPABLE OF KILLING THE COUPLE USING TAXPAYER FUNDED RESOURCES RIGHT NOW."*

read **NLRB-2020-000278** – *"THIS FOIA REQUEST IS BELIEVED TO CONTAIN DIRECT EVIDENCE OF THE MOTIVE, MEANS AND OPPORTUNITY FOR TWELVE (12) CURRENT NATIONAL LABOR RELATIONS BOARD EMPLOYEES TO COMMIT HIGH CRIMES AND MISDEMEANORS THAT INCLUDE <u>DEATH THREATS</u> AND MULTIPLE SEVERE VIOLA-*

TIONS OF THE LAW."

A Fraud Scheme Spanning Many Decades

Eric Marks *is a true creature of the Washington D.C. swamp. Despite lacking the skills, character, integrity and experience for this level of pay and responsibility,* **Eric Marks** *still receives over $162,000 per year plus federal benefits from U.S. taxpayers, and he has been paid over $2 million in total so-called 'compensation' from U.S. taxpayers during his government occupation.*

On April 4, 2016, I took a job at the **National Labor Relations Board** – *a.k.a.* NLRB, as the Associate Chief Information Officer for Enterprise Applications. I was hired under the Veteran's preference law as a disabled military veteran to run the agency's NxGen case management and reporting systems.

```
Within weeks of reporting to work, I uncovered obvious system
security vulnerabilities, wasteful spending totaling more than
$10 million, and contract fraud by the NLRB Chief Information
Officer Prem Aburvasamy and my predecessor Sivaram Ghorakavi who
had just left my job. I spent the next several months assembling
the records and auditing the contracts. I could not believe the
level of corruption and deceit involved. I raised these issues
constantly to the NLRB Chief Information Officer, Prem
Aburvasamy, and he ordered me to stand down. After I resisted,
he reassigned me to report to Eric Marks.
```

In my first meeting in November 2016, with my new supervisor Eric Marks, I explained in detail **Prem Aburvasamy's fraud scheme**, and **Eric Marks** told me that "military veterans and their styles of leadership are not welcome at NLRB." In that meeting, Eric Marks issued a threat.

> **Eric Marks** said that if I filed a formal Whistleblower complaint, he would personally ensure that I was retaliated against for blowing the whistle. He told me, "If you come after us, we are going to come after you!" with the arrogance of Peter Strzok.

Naturally, I was very disappointed to hear that the military principles that guided my entire life – integrity, honor and service to the nation – were not welcome at the NLRB and could get me fired. But I was on a mission to expose corruption in government if found, and so I decided to escalate the matter.

After meeting with **Eric Marks**, I reported my whistleblower complaints to the Inspector General **David Berry** using the Whistleblower hotline. I also made protected Whistleblower complaints about Aburvasamy's and Ghorakavi's illegal conduct to **Eric Marks** and the entire NLRB Board.

On November 30, 2016, I made a whistleblower complaint directly to all NLRB Board Members and the NLRB General Counsel. In that email with the subject *"Request for Help,"* I explained the situation and literally "begged" the NLRB Board Members and the NLRB General Counsel to halt the active retaliation that was being carried out against me by **Prem Aburvasamy** and **Eric Marks** for the protected whistleblower complaints that I had already made to Marks and the Inspector General.

The next day, on December 1, 2016 – one day after I sent the email to all the NLRB Board members complaining about **Prem Aburvasamy** and **Eric Marks**, the Inspector General **David Berry** launched a bogus investigation against me in retaliation for making my Whistleblower complaints. His job was to dig up any dirt he could to have me fired. He failed to produce anything, but that didn't stop **Elizabeth Bach** from doing what she does best: Fuck People Over.

The Deputy General Counsel at the time, **Jennifer Abruzzo**, was subsequently fired for coordinating the retaliation against me through **Eric Marks** and **Prem Aburvasamy** in order to conceal fraud at the NLRB.

According to Inspector General David Berry's own semi-annual report that he issued after I was terminated, the IG said, "We investigated a (false) allegation that a GS-15 level employee (John Edwards) threatened to take certain personnel actions against employees without just cause (John Edwards made protected Whistleblower complaints). We did not substantiate the allegation (against Mr. Edwards). We provided management with a summary of our investigative findings (and then Mr. Edwards was fired for blowing the whistle on corruption)."[1]

On the morning of February 7, 2017, when I reported to work – my government equipment was confiscated by **Eric Marks**. My network credentials were disabled, and I was escorted from my office located on the third floor at 1015 Half St SE, in Washington, D.C. by an armed uniformed security guard in full view of all NLRB staff and my peers who had been gathered in the hallway to watch me be shamefully escorted out of the building. This public display was cruelly carried out in order to defame my character, harm my reputation, and diminish my credibility as a witness against them. It also sent a signal to the entire workforce – blow the whistle and you will be fired!

Despite being ambushed and tossed from the building, I kept copies of all the reports, documents, and emails that I needed to prove my case in court. I also made recordings of some key meetings that support everything you have read in this article, and I made several Freedom of Information Act requests for the evidence I already had in my possession to protect the evidence and ensure it could not destroyed. Despite my efforts, senior officials including the NLRB Inspector General **David Berry** and FOIA Officer **Synta Keeling** were caught tampering with official government records, and despite their illegal and unethical conduct, both continue to be employed. Lucky for me, I still had the evidence that proved the entire NLRB leadership is corrupt.

I subsequently filed a lawsuit with the **Merit Systems Protection Board**, and the NLRB quickly settled with me and met all my demands in order to avoid accountability and publicity. I was awarded a settlement from the NLRB that was ratified on **May 18, 2017**. I was reinstated as a federal employee, paid back pay and leave, and reimbursed for all my legal expenses. I then promptly resigned from the agency on June 6, 2017. There was no way on earth that I could ever return to an agency that is so evil and corrupt. In the settlement I agreed to not file another complaint against the NLRB in exchange for me being allowed to publish my story.

After I won my case, **Sivaram Ghorakavi** was quickly hired back by **Prem Aburvasamy** to help him conceal his crimes. They are both part of the India mafia inside the federal government who use their corrupt influence in the United States and abroad for illegal profit.

The long reign of terror and corruption carried out by NLRB Inspector General **David Berry** has finally been recognized. **According to Bloomberg Law**, "The account of Ring's complaint against Inspector General David Berry was confirmed by three current and former senior agency personnel and four congressional staffers. They spoke with Bloomberg Law on condition of anonymity due to the sensitivity of the issue and because the complaint may still be pending at the Council of the Inspectors General on Integrity and Efficiency—which oversees IGs at federal agencies."

If President Trump's appointees at the NLRB do not act to **fire Eric Marks and the rest of his gang,** then the American people need to take matters into their own hands and make Whistleblower retaliation a Capital Crime.

Charles **Eric Marks** is a corrupt government bureaucrat who I believe must be terminated with extreme prejudice. With God's help, I will pray each day that **Eric Marks** is struck down by lightning and then tortured in Hell for what he has done to me. If Whistleblower Retaliation was a Capital Crime, then I would not have to pray that God kill this scumbag government bureaucrat – he would already be dead.

See the below court cases for material evidence to substantiate all allegations against named individuals in this article.

As of Labor Day 2020, the Department of Labor case decision is delayed because the MSPB doesn't have a quorum.

Evidence presented in that case is expected to show that Federal Deputy Chief Information Officer **Eric Marks'** former boss, **Jennifer Abruzzo**, acted on instructions from her close friend and former boss, *Department of Labor* executive **Lafe Solomon**, to have me fired for blowing the whistle at both agencies.

The evidence in the *Department of Labor case* will also demonstrate that Eric Marks' extremely low intelligence and lack of ethics in my view could be an unusable defense for him now that the court documents that won the NLRB case will be introduced at the Department of Labor trial.

That means I get to call NLRB witnesses.

I plan to expose the role of Prem Aburvasamy, Roxanne Rothschild and Synta Keeling in one of the most incredible U.S. government agency scandals in history. I intend to retaliate against the rotten scoundrels Hari Sharma and Ying Xing for their participation and lies.

All my evidence could take many years to be heard because of the backed-up court system and corrupt Department of Justice. It could even take decades for me to complete my retaliation against all the scumbags involved.

Nevertheless, I plan to continue to report this story until hell freezes over.

OPEN CASE:
U.S. Merit Systems Protection Board docket number
DC-1221-16-0227-W-1 / John S. Edwards v. Department of Labor

OTHER CASES:
U.S. Merit Systems Protection Board docket number

DC-0752-17-0467-I-1 / John S. Edwards v. National Labor Relations Board

Equal Employment Opportunity Commission case number

CLOSED: 570-2016-01154X / Agency No. 16-11-021

John Stuart Edwards v. SAIC / DoD Inspector General Case# 121468

> And I will continue to look forward to the day that all these
> government pieces of shit die. I will continue to pray for it,
> every single day I am alive. And I hope to be able to report
> about the end, of their lives.

NOTES

1. See United States Government, National Labor Relations Board Office of Inspector General, Semiannual Report October 1, 2016 – March 31, 2017, pg 4.

Prem Aburvasamy Takes NLRB Corruption To India

WHISTLEBLOWER NOTIFICATION

EMAIL SENT TO THE
NATIONAL LABOR RELATIONS BOARD
OFFICE OF THE INSPECTOR GENERAL
NLRB OFFICE OF CONGRESSIONAL AND PUBLIC AFFAIRS
NLRB GENERAL COUNSEL
NLRB FREEDOM OF INFORMATION ACT OFFICER

-----Original Message-----
From: IMIEJediMaster @ Capitol Hellway

To: OIGHOTLINE@nlrb.gov; publicinfo@nlrb.gov; peter.robb@nlrb.gov; Synta.Keeling@nlrb.gov
Sent: Fri, Mar 2, 2018 1:45 pm
Subject: Corruption continues at the NLRB under IG David Potts Berry

Prem Aburvasamy is accused of illegally selling U.S. government jobs to vulnerable foreign students on behalf of a private job placement firm for personal gain.

Read the article
Prem Aburvasamy Takes NLRB Corruption To India

Capitol Hellway Media Company LLC
A Free Media Company in the 21st Century

*This blog post is an official **Whistleblower Complaint** made on behalf of a **Whistleblower** who at this time has requested to remain anonymous.*

THE WHISTLEBLOWER COMPLAINT

Prem Aburvasamy is abusing his official U.S. federal government position again. This time, Aburvasamy stands accused of illegally selling U.S. government jobs to vulnerable foreign students on behalf of a private job placement firm for personal gain.

"The private placement agencies have made elaborate advertisements by erecting billboards in prominent places in the city depicting Prem Aburvasamy's federal government CIO title and the NLRB organization to lure job seekers to events where each attendee is required to pay $50.00 to hear Aburvasamy's speeches."

PAID ADVERTISEMENT ON STREETS OF INDIA FOR NLRB CHIEF INFORMATION OFFICER

According to the source, Prem Aburvasamy is receiving compensation and other benefits for speaking at these events including, *"wine, wealth and women"* in exchange for encouraging foreign students to participate in a U.S. job placement program that he personally guarantees on behalf of a private company.

Sources who attended his speeches say that **Prem Aburvasamy is using his current job in the United States federal government** as a credential **to guarantee job placement and immigrant work visas** for hundreds of students in India.

During a recent widely advertised speech at the Mount Zion International School in India, Prem Aburvasamy told the audience that he will use all his influence and power as a senior U.S. government executive on behalf of the private company. Prem Aburvasamy also told students that he can personally guarantee that each of the students who sign up for the program will obtain a job and work authorization in the United States of America. Several attendees say they are skeptical of his claims and appalled that he is being permitted by the NLRB to abuse his authority and steal money from the students by making false claims on behalf of a private company for personal gain.

Aburvasamy is the Chief Information Officer at the National Labor Relations Board, *a.k.a. NLRB*, and has been allowed to continue his government employment there despite being accused of committing criminal acts and whistleblower retaliation during the past year.

FREEDOM OF INFORMATION ACT REQUEST (FOIA)

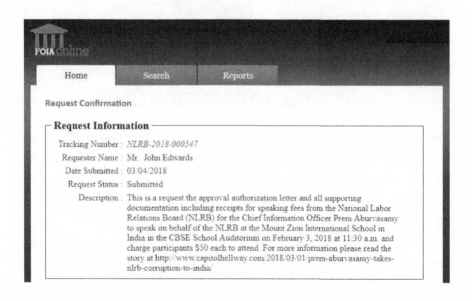

FREEDOM OF INFORMATION ACT REQUEST (FOIA)
NLRB RESPONSE

UNITED STATES GOVERNMENT
NATIONAL LABOR RELATIONS BOARD
FREEDOM OF INFORMATION ACT BRANCH
Washington, D.C. 20570

Via email

March 14, 2018

John Edwards
Capitol Hellway Media Company LLC
█████████████████

Re: FOIA Case No. NLRB-2018-000547

Dear Mr. Edwards:

This is in response to your request under the Freedom of Information Act (FOIA), 5 U.S.C. § 552, received in this Office on March 4, 2018, in which you request a copy of the approval authorization letter and all supporting documentation including receipts for speaking fees from the National Labor Relations Board for the Chief Information Officer to speak on behalf of the NLRB at a school in India on February 3, 2018.

We acknowledged your request on March 5, 2018.

Pursuant to the FOIA, a reasonable search was conducted by contacting the relevant Agency offices who might possess any responsive records. Specifically, searches inquiries were directed to the Office of Employee Development, the Office of the Chief Financial Officer/Travel Unit, and the Ethics Office. None of the searches conducted by these offices produced any records responsive to your request.

Sincerely,

Synta E. Keeling/s/

Synta E. Keeling
Freedom of Information Act Officer

This complaint was sent to the NLRB Inspector General Hotline in accordance with the procedures described on the agency's website that are pictured below.

NATIONAL LABOR RELATIONS BOARD

Home » Who We Are » Inspector General

Inspector General Hotline

Report violations of Laws and Regulations relating to NLRB Programs

Call:

- (800) 736-2983
- (202) 273-1960

Write:

- David P. Berry, Inspector General
  National Labor Relations Board
  1015 Half Street SE
  Washington, DC 20570-0001

Email:

- OIGHOTLINE@nlrb.gov

This Whistleblower complaint was sent by email to the Office of the Inspector General for the National Labor Relations Board and other officials on Friday, March 2, 2018 at 1:45 p.m.

Corruption at the National Labor Relations Board

National Labor Relations Board – *a.k.a.* **NLRB**

– *Six Updates* to this story have been published and are available below in descending order that provide evidence of death threats and attacks sanctioned by **NLRB Inspector General David Berry** and **Labor Inspector General Scott Dahl** against a federal government **Whistleblower** in Naples Florida. For court information, see the case:

```
John Stuart Edwards v. U. S. Department of Labor Docket Number
DC-1221-16-0227-W-1
```

UPDATE 6: February 13, 2020

READ MORE DIRECT EVIDENCE OF A COVER-UP by **Labor Inspector General Scott Dahl & NLRB Inspector General David Berry to Stop this Case:**

January 6 2020 Letter – NLRB Chairman to Council of the Inspectors General on Integrity and Efficiency

January 29 2020 Letter – NLRB Chairman to Council of the Inspectors General on Integrity and Efficiency

See FOIA Request Number **NLRB-2020-000480** for an evidentiary listing that proves additional crimes by the Council of the Inspectors General on Integrity and Efficiency and its members are being concealed.

Chapter 18. Deborah Jeffrey – Vice Chairperson – CIGIE

UPDATE 5: December 18, 2019

Chapter 19. The Edwards Dossier

UPDATE 4: November 14, 2019

Chapter 20. Killing NLRB Chairman John Ring

UPDATE 3: On Friday November 8, 2019 at noon,

National Labor Relations Board attorney Elizabeth Bach dispatched DHS-FPS agents in Florida to covertly enter private property in violation of the law for the second time in 23 months with direct orders to intimidate and violate the constitutional rights of the journalist who published reports of misconduct at the NLRB. Capitol Hellway Media Company has received a copy of a whistleblower complaint that is being circulated around the country and can be read here:

DHS AGENTS CAUGHT ON VIDEO VIOLATING THE FIRST AMENDMENT RIGHTS OF NAPLES FLORIDA JOURNALIST[1]

DHS AGENTS CAUGHT ON VIDEO VIOLATING THE FIRST AMENDMENT RIGHTS OF NAPLES FLORIDA JOURNALIST

We are here on orders from NLRB Attorney Elizabeth Bach to violate your constitutional rights & discourage you from publishing your book.

12:00 PM
Friday, November 8, 2019
Veteran's Day Holiday Weekend
POLICE DHS
Capitol Hellway Media Company LLC

UPDATE 2 – On October 3, 2019, John Stuart Edwards received a death threat letter in the U.S. postal service sent from Synta Keeling at the NLRB, and reported her threats of 'harassment and violence' to the FBI. The letter from Synta Keeling suggests that Mr. Edwards should "reasonably expect"

violence to happen soon for writing this article. John Stuart Edwards is a private citizen and journalist who for two years has written about corruption and malfeasance at the government agency that he witnessed by Synta Keeling. Keeling and the others at the agency who issued this threat should be arrested and punished to the fullest extent of the law.

UPDATE 1: September 29, 2019

Corruption at the National Labor Relations Board
August 30, 2019
by
John Stuart Edwards

The long reign of terror and corruption carried out by NLRB Inspector General David Berry has finally been recognized.

Now, the NLRB officials who have been operating under his protection – Prem Aburvasamy, Eric Marks, Elizabeth Bach, Roxanne Rothschild, Hari Sharma, Ying Xing, Sivaram Ghorakavi and Synta Keeling must all be fired too.

THE WHISTLEBLOWER COMPLAINTS

*"Inspector General **David Berry** is a narcissistic asshole who covered up evidence that proved beyond a reasonable doubt that NLRB officials under his protection – including the NLRB CIO **Prem Aburvasamy** and FOIA Officer **Synta Keeling**, conspired with criminal intent to conceal more than $10 million in cash from U.S. taxpayers," proclaimed John Stuart Edwards, the Whistleblower at the National Labor Relations Board who blew the lid off their illegal operations on **November 30, 2016.**

From: Edwards, John
Sent: Wednesday, November 30, 2016 9:03 AM
To: Pearce, Mark G. <Mark.Pearce@nlrb.gov>; Miscimarra, Philip A. <Philip.Miscimarra@nlrb.gov>; McFerran, Lauren <Lauren.McFerran@nlrb.gov>; Griffin, Richard F. <Richard.Griffin@nlrb.gov>

Subject: Request for Help

Good morning. My apologies for the intrusion but I have nowhere else to turn. I am your ACIO for Mission Systems which includes NxGen, JCMS and FTS, along with all your scanners and the reporting data warehouse. I joined the NLRB in April 2016 and have quietly done my very best to analyze, stabilize and improve your systems at a lower cost and have produced significant results in a very short time. I supervise 5 bargaining unit employees, and 4 GS14's along with about 10-12 contractors at this time and have made great strides to improving both productivity and morale.

There is a very severe management issue that is spiraling out of control in the OCIO that I feel requires very senior leadership intervention to resolve to protect the reputation of the NLRB and everyone involved. I respectfully request your assistance in resolving the matter internally and appropriately.

I think the attached communications explain the current situation well, which is deteriorating quickly into a hostile work environment for me and making me ill. I beg you to please ask my supervisor Eric Marks and the OCIO Prem Aburvasamy to halt their active retaliation of me until a proper independent investigation into the totality and validity of all the complaints involved can be done.

Exhibit A: Edwards Whistleblower Complaint to Entire NLRB Board

John Stuart Edwards has publicly called for *David Berry* and the others to be fired since 2016, after he officially reported their malfeasance. Edwards uncovered *Prem Aburvasamy's* organized crime operation that extends to India within weeks of his arrival at the agency, and was humiliated and fired after making this report to *Chairman Miscimarra* on *November 30, 2016.*

According to Edwards, "Working at the NLRB was surreal. At times, I imagined that I was working for the mafia. The NLRB has two classes of employees who work there. The workers who are too afraid to blow the whistle, and the executives who are too corrupt to be held accountable."[2]

HOW DAVID BERRY GOT CAUGHT

On **May 30, 2019**, I sent documentation of the crimes committed by **David Berry** to his supervisor – the new NLRB **Chairman John Ring**. I also notified my Florida congressman *Mario Díaz-Balart* who immediately investigated the matter.[3]

On **June 26, 2019**, *Bloomberg Law reported* that NLRB **Chairman John Ring** had filed a formal complaint against his Inspector General **David Berry** to have him fired. According to the report, Ring's complaint concerns Berry's harsh treatment of agency employees and other complaints that have been filed against the inspector general in the past few years.

According to Bloomberg Law, "The account of Ring's complaint against Inspector General David Berry was confirmed by three current and former senior agency personnel and four congressional staffers. They spoke with Bloomberg Law on condition of anonymity due to the sensitivity of the issue and because the complaint may still be pending at the Council of the Inspectors General on Integrity and Efficiency—which oversees IGs at federal agencies."

There is a long-documented history of widespread corruption at the NLRB that Inspector General **David Berry** has either refused to investigate or covered up. David Berry has falsified and tampered with official government records, denied documents requested under FOIA – The Freedom of Information Act – and retaliated against Whistleblowers.

Here is one recent example of an evasive and arrogant response that **David Berry** provided to a public request for documentation related to his crimes.

United States Government

NATIONAL LABOR RELATIONS BOARD

OFFICE OF INSPECTOR GENERAL

Washington, DC 20570-0001

February 21, 2019

This letter is in response to your Freedom of Information Act requests:

The OIG neither admits nor denies the existence of the information you seek because any such confirmation or denial would harm the interests of the NLRB.

Sincerely,

James E. Tatum, Jr.

James E. Tatum, Jr.
Counsel to the Inspector General

The multiple complaints made against NLRB Inspector General **David Berry** have never been fully investigated or resolved, until now.

THE ORIGINS OF THIS DRAMA

Jennifer Abruzzo and officials at the **Department of Labor** conspired to retaliate against me for blowing the whistle at both agencies.

Just one day after my formal complaint was filed with his office on **November 30, 2016, David Berry** retaliated against me for blowing the whistle and had me fired for speaking up. I subsequently sued the NLRB and was awarded damages for Berry's bad acts. See U.S. Merit Systems Protection Board docket number DC-0752-17-0467-I-1 / John S. Edwards v. National Labor Relations Board / for case documents and material evidence to substantiate all allegations against named individuals in this article.

Jennifer Abruzzo was fired and here is why.

Former Deputy General Counsel Jennifer Abruzzo allegedly conspired with her close friend and former boss, Department of Labor executive **Lafe Solomon**, a very controversial figure who was considered by Watchdog.org to be one of the Scariest People in 2016.

In legal terms, this meeting between Solomon and Abruzzo created a nexus between the retaliation that I suffered at the Department of Labor and my treatment by Abruzzo and Prem Aburvasamy at its sister agency, the NLRB.

The case against the **Department of Labor** is still awaiting action by the courts and you can read all about that here.

According to sources, Abruzzo & Solomon held a meeting in 2016 and decided to work together to have me fired for reporting systemic racism at the Department of Labor. "Doing whatever it takes," to get me fired was discussed.

And then they carried it out. These affidavits and other evidence will be introduced at trial after appropriate discovery is completed at both agencies.

The article *"Killing Whistleblower Retaliators at the NLRB"* explains why **Phillip Miscimarra** departed the federal government at the end of his term as the **Chairman of the National Labor Relations Board** on December

16, 2017, despite being asked by President Trump to serve another term.

REVENGE, SWEET REVENGE

"Metaphorically, if the victims of sexual assault are
whistleblowers, then I was gang-raped by Phillip Miscimarra,"
said John Stuart Edwards, a Whistleblower for the National Labor
Relations Board. "It disgusts me that this piece of shit —
Miscimarra — presided over U.S. labor law disputes impacting
millions of workers across the country while he was retaliating
against me. He should have been fired sooner!"

So far, my reporting has resulted in the **removal of the former NLRB Chairman Phillip Miscimarra and the firing of the former Deputy General Counsel Jennifer Abruzzo and an investigation into the Inspector General.** With any luck, the other co-conspirators – Prem Aburvasamy, Eric Marks, Elizabeth Bach, Roxanne Rothschild, Hari Sharma, Ying Xing, Sivaram Ghorakavi and Synta Keeling will all be fired too.

Revenge is indeed a dish best served cold, and I feel an extreme warmth at the prospect that **David Berry** will finally be held accountable, and then sentenced by God when he dies to an eternity in Hell where he will burn in pain, forever.[4]

NOTES

1. The video is being reviewed for possible use in a documentary about government corruption and unlawful conduct that will be published to promote the *Petition to the Government for a Redress of Grievances,* **a.k.a.** "The Edwards Dossier" textbook.
2. See "Obama pick for NLRB was top lawyer for union tainted by mob ties, history of corruption."
3. **John Ring** was appointed by President Trump on April 12, 2018.

The purpose of this chapter is to create a permanent record of the crimes committed by government officials against American Citizens that I witnessed. My primary objective is to retaliate against those who retaliated against me by publicly exposing who they are for all time. All named individuals in this article and the agencies involved were contacted and provided many months/years to comment before publication. All written communications with government agencies and documentation supporting all allegations contained in this textbook are fully described herein.

Punishing Corruption at the NLRB

Two FOIA requests provide readers with all the direct evidence needed for the U.S. government to fire & prosecute TWELVE (12) CURRENT NATIONAL LABOR RELATIONS BOARD EMPLOYEES, including NLRB Inspector General David Berry.

read **NLRB-2020-000275** – "ALL RECIPIENTS OF THIS 'REQUEST FOR INFORMATION' ARE ADVISED TO CONTACT LAW ENFORCEMENT OFFICIALS IMMEDIATELY UPON READING THIS 'REQUEST FOR INFORMATION' TO REPORT THAT YOU HAVE RECEIVED FACTUAL EVIDENCE ABOUT A THREAT OF VIOLENCE MADE AGAINST TWO AMERICAN CITIZENS IN NAPLES FLORIDA BY SENIOR U.S. GOVERNMENT OFFICIALS WHO STILL REMAIN CAPABLE OF KILLING THE COUPLE USING TAXPAYER FUNDED RESOURCES RIGHT NOW."

read **NLRB-2020-000278** – "THIS FOIA REQUEST IS BELIEVED TO CONTAIN DIRECT EVIDENCE OF THE MOTIVE, MEANS AND OPPORTUNITY FOR TWELVE (12) CURRENT NATIONAL LABOR RELATIONS BOARD EMPLOYEES TO COMMIT HIGH CRIMES AND MISDEMEANORS THAT INCLUDE DEATH THREATS AND MULTI-PLE SEVERE VIOLATIONS OF THE LAW."

Inside the National Labor Relations Board in Washington D.C., Inspector General David Berry's reputation as a deep state bureaucrat is widely known and respected by his corrupt peers at the Council of Inspectors General on Integrity and Efficiency. When I met with IG David Berry during our interviews for OIG-I-530 Report Dated January 3, 2017, he bragged to me about how he really missed his old job working with the U.S. Marine Corps where he said he investigated and prosecuted military officers. He seemed delighted by the idea. He said it gave him a sense of power. In my opinion, this guy is a narcissist-nut-job who should be fired immediately.

THIS INSPECTOR GENERAL SHOULD BE FIRED!
NLRB INSPECTOR GENERAL **DAVID POTTS BERRY**
SHUTS DOWN WHISTLEBLOWER HOTLINE!

There is a long history at the National Labor Relations Board, *a.k.a. NLRB,* of corruption that Inspector General **David Potts Berry** has refused to investigate in order to protect his radical friends and neighbors who work at the agency. I personally witnessed the falsification and tampering with official government records by David Potts Berry, and filed complaints against him with the corrupt officials at the agency who were in charge at the time which were never investigated or resolved.

Here are two examples of complaints from my investigation into corruption at the agency that, as of today, were never investigated and are are no longer available to the public because the Inspector General David Potts Berry shut down the Whistleblower Hotline. Good thing I kept screenshots.

Submission #187
Submission #197

THE SOURCES OF INSPECTOR GENERAL DAVID BERRY'S PROTECTION

Read all about the Corruption at the Council of Inspectors General on Integrity and Efficiency

PHILIP A. MISCIMARRA

Two senior U.S. government officials have resigned from the federal government for corruption, contract fraud and discriminating against a disabled Veteran after being caught carrying out illegal *Prohibited Personnel Practices* to retaliate against a whistleblower in violation of the law.[1]

CORRUPT GOVERNMENT OFFICIALS

PHILIP A. MISCIMARRA | JENNIFER A. ABRUZZO

Sources believe that former National Labor Relations Board Chairman **Phillip Miscimarra** and Deputy General Counsel **Jennifer Abruzzo** were fired for retaliating against a whistleblower who reported government waste, fraud and abuse.[2]

The punishment for Philip Miscimarra's involvement in whistleblower retaliation became known this week after it was announced that he returned to same old jobs he held before his nearly five-year fling on the National Labor Relations Board.

At **the law firm Morgan Lewis,** Miscimarra returned to lead the firm's NLRB special appeals practice that assists clients with appeals to the board and its general counsel. Miscimarra will also resume his former role as senior fellow at the Center for Human Resources at the University of Pennsylvania's Wharton Business School.

The scandal is still being investigated by the Department of Justice (DOJ).[3] *For more on Abruzzo, scroll down to **JENNIFER ABRUZZO REJECTED FOR BOARD POSITION** in the **UPDATES**... section of this article to see how whistleblower retaliator **Jennifer Abruzzo got fired**. Also, read the chapter, "Jennifer Abruzzo Fired from NLRB" for the gritty details about Abruzzo's final workday at the NLRB and her abrupt departure from government employment under a dark cloud of corruption charges and abuse of power.*

Request for Information

From: Capitol Hellway Media Company LLC

Date: Wed, Feb 21, 2018 at 8:43 PM

Subject: Journalist Question for Public Affairs

To: publicinfo@nlrb.gov

Good evening,

Your agency stopped allowing anonymous whistleblower complaints today on its website and there was no explanation posted at the time I sent this request.

Question: Has NLRB Inspector General David Potts Berry suspended the use of an online automated hotline system that allows complaints to be submitted, tracked and posted online for the public to see?

A written response to this question is requested along with explanations that I can share with the public, and can be emailed to me directly at xxx@capitolhellway.com.

Also, if you would like to offer any additional comments about the series that I have published recently about your agency please provide that as well.

The multi-part series begins at this link:
http://www.capitolhellway.com/2017/11/30/killing-whistleblower-retaliators-nlrb/

The series consists of four articles at this moment, with many, many more planned and in the pipes.

If you have any questions emails are preferred, however do please call or text me anytime if required by federal law.

Sincerely,
John Stuart Edwards
Capitol Hellway Media Company, LLC
http://www.capitolhellway.com/

The Department of Homeland Security and the NLRB refuse to respond to all *Capitol Hellway Media Company LLC* requests for comment on the matter.[4]

Shirley McKay / Correspondence Management Analyst / Office of Legislative Affairs at the U.S. Department of Justice stated in an email on January 8 that, *"After the review is completed a written response will be sent..."*

THE BOUNTY...

a sum paid for killing or capturing a person or animal

Hi. My name is Johnny. I am a whistleblower. My goal in writing these articles is to cast bright sunshine on the corrupt people who retaliate against whistleblowers, and then discover creative new ways to ensure that these parasites are severely punished and destroyed. **Please read more about my writing here.**

IMAGINATION IS WHERE FACT AND FICTION COLLIDE

"I was retaliated against and fired from my government job for blowing the whistle on two corrupt bureaucrats who are still permitted to hold a federal government job."

The DOJ is currently investigating senior NLRB officials after I complained to Congressman Mario Diaz-Balart (R-FL).[5]

In the next stage of reporting for this story, I intend to raise the voltage a bit on the two federal employees that I blew the whistle on, and their two loyal accomplices. These people need to be placed on a **target list** for immediate removal from the U.S. federal government workforce by any means necessary.

After removal, these people should all be banned from working for any U.S. federal agency or contractor for the rest of their lives. These parasitic bastards should also be prohibited from voting or holding public office.

"To me and a growing number of other moral people from around the world, this type of punishment is only a fraction of what these animals deserve for the pain and suffering they caused me and my family."

I will want to pray each morning now;
that they all suffer a horrible and painful death.
I will want to fantasize in my dreams;
that they are all stripped, and beaten with a baseball bat;
and then chained alive to the back of a fast car.
I will want to visualize each of them in slow motion
being dragged down a gravel road at high speed.
To see the fear and dread in their faces.
And then watch them being dragged on a paved parking lot
while the car is doing donuts,
until their skulls crack open and their brains
spill out into a big circle of blood.
DEAD OR ALIVE[6]

*The **First Amendment to the U.S. Constitution** allows American Citizens to*

create and publish poetry and satirical art about what they want to pray about, or what they want to dream about. Mixing reality with poetic satire as a metaphor in this way is intended to help steer public imagination to a policy to punish whistleblower retaliators so severely that no one in the future will ever consider doing it again.

The bottom line is that Prem Aburvasamy and Eric Marks I believe broke the law and retaliated against me when I blew the whistle on them to the entire leadership of the National Labor Relations Board, *a.k.a. NLRB*.

On November 30, 2016, I made a written protected whistleblower complaint to the NLRB General Counsel, the Inspector General David Potts Berry and the entire Board at the NLRB, including the **Chairman Philip A. Miscimarra**. In an email with the subject *"Request for Help,"* I complained that my current working environment was hostile. I literally "begged" them to halt the active retaliation that was being carried out against me by Aburvasamy and Marks for making protected whistleblower complaints.

From: Edwards, John
Sent: Wednesday, November 30, 2016 9:03 AM
To: Pearce, Mark G. <Mark.Pearce@nlrb.gov>; Miscimarra, Philip A. <Philip.Miscimarra@nlrb.gov>; McFerran, Lauren <Lauren.McFerran@nlrb.gov>; Griffin, Richard F. <Richard.Griffin@nlrb.gov>
Subject: Request for Help

Good morning. My apologies for the intrusion but I have nowhere else to turn. I am your ACIO for Mission Systems which includes NxGen, JCMS and FTS, along with all your scanners and the reporting data warehouse. I joined the NLRB in April 2016 and have quietly done my very best to analyze, stabilize and improve your systems at a lower cost and have produced significant results in a very short time. I supervise 5 bargaining unit employees, and 4 GS14's along with about 10-12 contractors at this time and have made great strides to improving both productivity and morale.

There is a very severe management issue that is spiraling out of control in the OCIO that I feel requires very senior leadership intervention to resolve to protect the reputation of the NLRB and everyone involved. I respectfully request your assistance in resolving the matter internally and appropriately.

I think the attached communications explain the current situation well, which is deteriorating quickly into a hostile work environment for me and making me ill. I beg you to please ask my supervisor Eric Marks and the OCIO Prem Aburvasamy to halt their active retaliation of me until a proper independent investigation into the totality and validity of all the complaints involved can be done.

Hari Sharma and Ying Xing are two of the most dishonest and emotionally disturbed government bureaucrats I have ever met in my life. Sharma and Xing were named as accomplices in the whistleblower retaliation lawsuit I filed against the NLRB on April 25, 2017.[7]

As his former supervisor, I think that it is fair to say that GS-14 **Hari Sharma** is a mediocre software developer who immigrated to the U.S. with antiquated technology skills and no ambition for learning American values. It was clear to me that Hari Sharma hates America. When he worked for me, Hari Sharma complained constantly about how he bought his house at the top of the bubble and was underwater on his mortgage and really needed to find a way to get more money. Sharma stated that if he could sell his home and break even on the sale, he would move back to India as quickly as possible because he hates Americans, especially White people. Obviously, given his poor character and deep hatred for Americans and the fact that he sucks at software development, well, it doesn't take very long for a highly skilled software development manager to see that Hari Sharma is just a worthless federal government worker who immigrated to the U.S. to feed like a parasite on American taxpayer money at the expense of Americans who want to live and work in this country.

Ying Xing shares Sharma's hatred for Americans and they are very close friends. As her former supervisor, I would describe **Ying Xing** to a prospective employer as a very emotionally unstable and immature person. Ying Xing is an immigrant with very weak English speaking skills and low reading comprehension who is often very confused in conversations. In terms of her job performance, possibly due to the language barrier, Ying Xing really hasn't got a clue what she is doing and has no business being paid as a GS-14.

In my experiences, Hari Sharma and Ying Xing have the skills to perform at about the GS-7 level, not the GS-14 level that they are both paid. Sharma and Xing are being overpaid by taxpayers a total of about $200,000 per year in total compensation combined, and together rake in over $300,000 per year from American taxpayers.

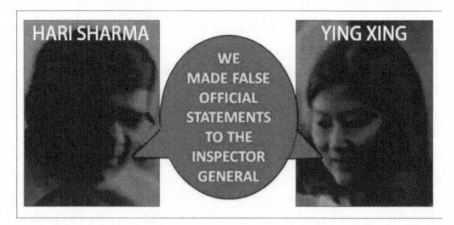

The legal problem for **Hari Sharma** and **Ying Xing** is that they made false official statements to the Inspector General David Potts Berry that are contained in a memorandum he issued on January 3, 2017.[8] Proof supported by material evidence that the two lied will be published later in this series. This series is based on many documents, some contained in the lawsuit case records described in *footnote 7*, FOIA requests and other sources.

I think that these four incompetent and morally bankrupt federal government bureaucrats should be clutched at the collar and tossed into prison where they can find out what it is like to be gang-raped![9]

It must be stated that Aburvasamy and Marks are not the brightest bulbs by any measure, and they do continue to protect powerful people in the government. It is entirely possible that these two are too stupid to know that they are no longer being protected by their bosses.

I have a message for them. Don't get comfortable!

HERE IS THE BOUNTY

I reported that Prem Aburvasamy and Eric Marks wasted more than $10 million in taxpayer money, and that Eric Marks has been paid over $2 million in compensation from U.S. taxpayers during his tenure with one federal agency. My complaint stated that Aburvasamy and Marks continue to engage in contract fraud to protect long-tenured federal government bureaucrats. For example, Jennifer Abruzzo, a 23 year veteran of the agency, was fired less than one month after I published the article, ***Killing Whistleblower Retaliators at the NLRB***, the first story in this series about corruption at the NLRB.[10]

There is only one major obstacle remaining now to eliminating fraudulent and wasteful spending by the United States federal government.

We must identify and then exterminate, eliminate, and eradicate the incompetent long-tenured career bureaucrats in Washington D.C. that waste taxpayer money and retaliate against Whistleblowers. These are people, like Prem Aburvasamy, Eric Marks, Hari Sharma and Ying Xing that view abuse of authority and deceit as a way of life.

As a result of the overwhelming evidence against them, Prem Aburvasamy, Eric Marks, Hari Sharma and Ying Xing have all been nominated by *Whistleblower Underground* to be placed on the official **international target list** for removal from the U.S. federal government workforce by any legal means necessary.

I believe that a fair punishment for these parasites is to use all legal means necessary to destroy their lives.

UPDATES...

on punishing corruption at the NLRB

JENNIFER ABRUZZO REJECTED FOR BOARD POSITION

Bloomberg Law reported on February 8, 2018, that Jennifer Abruzzo was in fact recommended for a vacant regional director position in Baltimore late last year by **former NLRB Chairman Phillip Miscimarra,** ostensibly as a reward for retaliating against me, and that she was turned down for the job by the Office of Personnel Management after her ties to corruption at the agency were exposed.

Jennifer Abruzzo started a new job last week at the Communications Workers of America Union, one month after being fired. According to the Bloomberg Law article, Abruzzo will be the union's point person on National Labor Relations Board issues at its headquarters in Washington, D.C.

The revolving door in government to the private sector still works well, and this union job for Abruzzo is certainly a step down from what she expected. Probably a favor to her to keep quiet. Hopefully her career never recovers.

DEPARTMENT OF JUSTICE INVESTIGATION

DHS Case Number N17003708: On December 6, 2017, a DHS agent and Sheriff's counterintelligence officer came to my home in Florida after I published a story about corruption and Whistleblower retaliation at the National Labor Relations Board. The agents told my wife and me that we should *"be careful"* and contact them if we see anything unusual like our *"cats getting killed"* or sudden vandalism at our home. They said that they were just, *"doing what some SES in Washington ordered,"* referring to Prem Aburvasamy who works at the agency. I recorded the meeting. The two agents asked and I agreed to not publish the recording or reveal their identities online because they said that they fear retaliation if I publish their names together with the details of our conversation. They seemed like good men who were just following ridiculous orders from parasitic bureaucrats in Washington D.C.

According to a letter dated February 7, 2018, from Congressman Mario Diaz-Balart, the Department of Justice is still reviewing the conduct of Prem Aburvasamy, Eric Marks and other NLRB officials including the Inspector General David Berry and Freedom of Information Act Officer Synta Keeling who are all involved in the complaint.

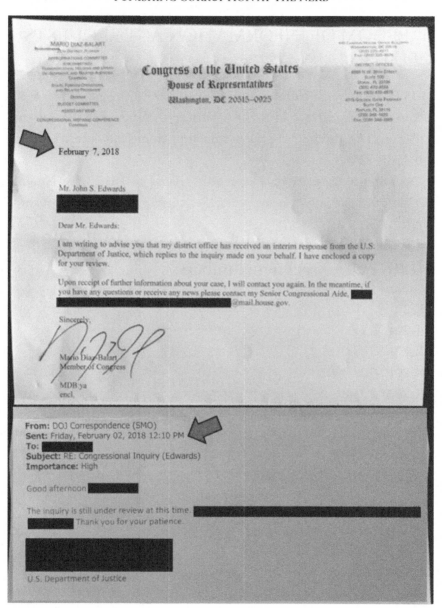

MARIO DIAZ-BALART

Congress of the United States
House of Representatives
Washington, DC 20515-0025

February 7, 2018

Mr. John S. Edwards

Dear Mr. Edwards:

I am writing to advise you that my district office has received an interim response from the U.S. Department of Justice, which replies to the inquiry made on your behalf. I have enclosed a copy for your review.

Upon receipt of further information about your case, I will contact you again. In the meantime, if you have any questions or receive any news please contact my Senior Congressional Aide, █████████ @mail.house.gov.

Sincerely,

Mario Diaz-Balart
Member of Congress

MDB ya
encl.

From: DOJ Correspondence (SMO)
Sent: Friday, February 02, 2018 12:10 PM
To: ████████
Subject: RE: Congressional Inquiry (Edwards)
Importance: High

Good afternoon █████████

The inquiry is still under review at this time. ██████████████████████
████████ Thank you for your patience.

U.S. Department of Justice

FREEDOM OF INFORMATION ACT REQUESTS UPDATE

<u>**DHS FOIA Request Number**</u>: 2018-NPFO-000152 (response received)

Rochelle Carpenter / FPS FOIA Officer / National Protection and Programs Directorate / U.S. Department of Homeland Security / Desk: (703) 235-2211

Documents Requested: all records related to DHS Case Number N17003708 including all forms, notes, files, correspondence, phone records, etc.

NLRB FOIA Tracking Numbers:

LR-2017-1152

LR-2017-1264

LR-2017-1283

LR-2017-1297

LR-2017-1313

APPEAL Letter LR-2017-1152

DHS FOIA Request Number: 2018-NPFO-000152

NLRB-2018-000547

Synta Keeling / NLRB FOIA Officer / Phone: (202) 273-2995 / Email: Synta.Keeling@nlrb.gov

Office of the Under Secretary
National Protection and Programs Directorate
U.S. Department of Homeland Security
Washington, DC 20528

February 27, 2018

SENT VIA EMAIL TO:

Mr. John Edwards

█████████████████

RE: 2018-NPFO-00152

Dear Mr. Edwards:

This is our response to your December 7, 2017, Freedom of Information Act (FOIA) request to
the Department of Homeland Security (DHS), National Protection and Programs Directorate
(NPPD). You are seeking a copy of incident report CCN N17003708 and documents related to
this incident report.

FEDERAL PROTECTIVE SERVICE
** FOR OFFICIAL USE ONLY **

Narrative Continuation

```
2017-12-12 10:55:45.253
On 12/6/17, I, Senior Special Agent (b) (6), (b) (7)(C), (k)(2)            with the Collier County
Sheriff's Office, conducted an interview of John EDWARDS (DOB:          ). Deputy (b) (6), and I conducted
the interview of EDWARDS at his residence, located at                  Naples, FL 34114.  At the
outset of the interview, I asked for permission for Deputy (b) (6), and I to enter EDWARDS' home and
EDWARDS allowed us enter his residence in order to speak with him.  During the interview, EDWARDS' (b) (6), (b)
(b) (6), (b) (7)(C), was present.  Additionally, EDWARDS asked to audio record the interview, and I explained
to him that he had every right to record the interview since it was taking place in his home.  The sum
and substance of the interview follows:

I explained to EDWARDS that I was at his house to speak with him about an allegation that he, EDWARDS,
had made threats towards several employees who work for the National Labor Relations Board (NLRB) in
Washington, DC.  I further explained to EDWARDS that (b) (7)(C), (b) (7)(F)
(b) (7)(C), (b) (7)(F)            in a "Wanted - Dead or Alive" type poster image.  EDWARDS admitted to
posting the image online as part the article he published online.  EDWARDS detailed how his article was
about his experiences as a "whistleblower."

I asked EDWARDS if he had any intention of harming the individuals portrayed in the image.  EDWARDS
stated that he had no intentions of causing any harm to either of the individuals.  EDWARDS stated that
he included the image in his posting for the dramatic effect.

During the interview, EDWARDS asked how the Department of Homeland Security (DHS) came to be involved in
investigating him.  I explained to EDWARDS that I was merely there following up on the allegation made by
(b) (6), (b) (7)(C)      EDWARDS stated that he felt that (b) (6), (b) (7)(C)                were
merely attempting to use DHS to harass him.  I advised EDWARDS that we follow up on allegations just like
any other law enforcement agency that handles cases of this nature.

At the end of the interview, I provided EDWARDS with the case control number for this case.  I also
provided EDWARDS with my business card.  EDWARDS asked if he could post an image of my business card on
the Internet.  I advised EDWARDS that since I had given him my card, he was free to post an image of it
online.  I then asked EDWARDS to censor my specific contact information from the image, if he chose to
post an image of my business card on his website.  EDWARDS agreed to censor my contact information out of
the image.  I also asked EDWARDS if he would refrain from posting the audio recording of the interview
on his website.  EDWARDS agreed to refrain from posting the audio recording of the interview on his
website.

At the end of the interview, EDWARDS provided me with his phone number (          ).  During the entire
interview, EDWARDS was cordial and oriented to person, place and time.  During the entire interview,
EDWARDS' thoughts were organized and he had no issues articulating those thoughts.
```

Sincerely,

T. Fuentes

T. Fuentes
Director, FOIA
National Protection and Programs Directorate

The National Labor Relations Board refused to respond to our Freedom of
Information Act requests in violation of 5 U.S.C. § 552. And then the death
threats arrived at our businesses via the U.S. mail.

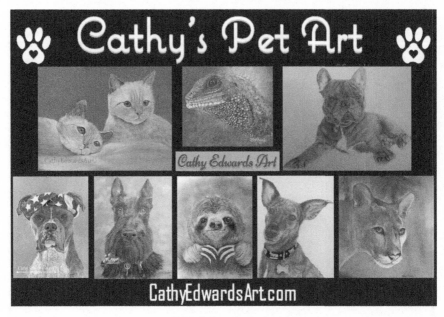

Free Advertisement

For the record, I do not intend to murder Washington swamp creatures Aburvasamy, Marks, Sharma and Xing. I only want to see their lives destroyed.

If you want to participate in their destruction, please send me your ideas about how to make these morally bankrupt bureaucrats legally suffer for all the pain they inflicted upon me for being a whistleblower.[11]

Contact Me
PUBLISH YOUR STORY!
Internet records can last a long time and are easily searchable.
Believe in KARMA
Severe punishment for whistleblower retaliators is finally available to US.

NOTES

1. See **5 USC § 2302**

2. **This article explains** why Phillip Miscimarra, who was appointed by President Obama departed the federal government at the end of his term as the Chairman of the National Labor Relations Board on December 16, 2017, despite being asked by President Trump to serve another term.

3. See **DEPARTMENT OF JUSTICE INVESTIGATION** in the **UPDATES...** section of this article for the current status of the **NLRB corruption and fraud investigation**.

4. See **FREEDOM OF INFORMATION ACT REQUESTS UPDATE** in the **UPDATES...** section of this article for the current status of FOIA requests in this case.

5. See **DEPARTMENT OF JUSTICE INVESTIGATION** in the **UPDATES...** section of this article for the current status of the **NLRB corruption and fraud investigation**.

6. A poem by John Stuart Edwards

7. See U.S. Merit Systems Protection Board docket number DC-0752-17-0467-I-1 / John S. Edwards v. National Labor Relations Board / for case documents and material evidence to substantiate all allegations against named individuals in this article.

8. NLRB Inspector General David Potts Berry is a pathetic example of a government watchdog and should be fired too, but more on that later.

9. Metaphorically speaking, of course. If the victims of sexual assault are whistleblowers, then I was gang-raped by these people.

10. Read how **Jennifer Abruzzo was rejected for a Board position** in the **UPDATES...** section of this article.

11. Metaphorically speaking, broad exaggerations and satire are welcome of course. **Nothing suggested that is illegal will ever be carried out!**

Jennifer Abruzzo Fired from NLRB

After almost twenty-three years as a government bureaucrat, Jennifer Abruzzo was asked to resign or be fired from the National Labor Relations Board (NLRB) located in Washington D.C. after an investigation was threatened by the Department of Justice into her alleged immoral and unethical conduct as a government employee. According to two sources at the NLRB who worked for Abruzzo, her announcement was, "*a last minute decision*," and, "*she did not say where she was headed.*"

THE CASE AGAINST ABRUZZO, ABURVASAMY AND MARKS

Capitol Hellway published the story on November 30, 2017, *Killing Whistle-blower Retaliators at the NLRB* – that chronicled Ms. Abruzzo's personal involvement with corruption and Whistleblower retaliation at the small federal government agency.

In an email interview request sent to Ms. Abruzzo's supervisor on December 3, 2017, NLRB General Counsel Peter B. Robb was informed that *"The focus of [the next] article is either going to be Abruzzo's retention by you, or her dismissal/departure."*

Three days later on December 6, 2017, *Capitol Hellway* reported in the article, *Killing Prem Aburvasamy and Eric Marks* – that sources close to Abruzzo said she was planning to remain at the NLRB, *and* that the Department of Justice was asked by Congressman Mario Diaz-Balart (R-FL) to investigate the NLRB's General Counsel Peter B. Robb, Jennifer Abruzzo, Prem Aburvasamy and Eric Marks for abuse of authority and for violating an investigative journalist's Constitutional Rights.

REVENGE IS A DISH BEST SERVED COLD

On a frigid Friday afternoon in late December – on the eve of the New Year's Day government holiday weekend while the majority of federal workers were on leave – Abruzzo's long tenure at the NLRB came to an abrupt and unceremonious end.

In an email obtained exclusively by *Capitol Hellway Media Company LLC*, Jennifer Abruzzo informed the entire organization that she was leaving the NLRB. The hastily prepared email was sent to the entire NLRB workforce, contained misspelled words, and provided no explanation about Abruzzo's apparent unplanned departure from the agency.

EMAIL FROM: JENNIFER ABRUZZO
TO: ALL NLRB Personnel
Friday, December 29, 2017

Today is my last workday at the NLRB.

One of the greatest highlights of my life has been my tenure at this amazing and unique Agency. I feel so very fortunate to have worked side by side with such talented, innovative and dedicated individuals. No matter what position you hold, you help to effectuate the mission of this Agency, and for that I am eternally grateful. Protecting workers' rights is one of the most important contributions that we can make to this country and even more broadly. I know that you will continue to wirk tirelessly info educating workers, unions, employers and the general public about the Act and in promoting industrial peace and stability in workplaces nationwide. I am proud to be part of the NLRB family and I thank you for your friendship, collaboration, advice, guidance and support overt the years. I wish you and your families all the very best. I will miss you.

Take care,
Jennifer

Multiple sources confirmed that there was no advance warning given about Abruzzo's departure. There were no meetings held, no "*farewell parties" planned, and no discreet collections for any gifts or a plaque. There were no gatherings of employees to make the announcement or luncheons scheduled to see her off, despite the fact that Abruzzo worked at the NLRB for almost twenty-three years and the majority of the organization worked directly for her. Abruzzo's sudden departure without a formal sendoff or new job announcement was characterized by one worker as, *"very unusual and suspicious."*

*UPDATE: On March 6, 2018 the NLRB held a farewell event for Abruzzo. This event took place more than 60 days after her firing. All NLRB employees were invited to attend the event. According to sources inside the agency, this party was organized in response to this article.

NO TRANSPARENCY OR ACCOUNTABILITY

NLRB General Counsel Peter B. Robb did not respond to multiple requests for interviews for this article and the NLRB Public Affairs Office /Phone: 202-273-1991/ Email: publicinfo @nlrb.gov has ignored all formal requests for information.

SYNTA KEELING
NLRB FOIA BRANCH CHIEF

NLRB FOIA Officer Synta Keeling / *Phone*: (202) 273-2995 / *Email*: Synta.Keeling@nlrb.gov refuses to respond to Freedom of Information Act requests in violation of 5 U.S.C. § 552.[1]

Synta Keeling has also willfully and unlawfully concealed government records from the public in violation of U.S. Code Title 18, Section 2071, and there is evidence that she conspired with the NLRB Inspector General David Potts Berry, Special Counsel Elizabeth Bach, CIO Prem Aburvasamy and Eric Marks to tamper with document requests and alter official government records in order to conceal corruption at the agency.[2]

LIFE GOES ON

In the wake of Abruzzo's resignation, NLRB's General Counsel Peter B. Robb named John W. Kyle to fill Abruzzo's position as his Deputy General Counsel. In an email sent to the entire workforce this week, Robb wrote, *"John [Kyle] brings more than 40 years of professional experience to our Agency. He began his career as an Equal Opportunity Specialist with the Department of Defense, and later went on to the Federal Labor Relations Agency as a Labor Relations Specialist and Field Attorney, law firms handling cases on behalf of employers and individuals, and our very own Agency – having served as a Field Examiner in region 5 and later as Counsel and Senior Counsel to former NLRB member Robert P. Hunter until 1985."*

There was no mention in Mr. Robb's email about Abruzzo's departure from the agency, nor was there any praise for her more than twenty years government employment at the NLRB. At the publication of this article, the official NLRB website contained no news releases or announcements of Kyle's appointment or Abruzzo's departure.

AGENCY RESPONSE

At 1:16 PM on January 11, 2018 the following email message was delivered to the NLRB General Counsel Peter B. Robb:

Subject: Press Inquiry

To: peter.robb @nlrb.gov

Mr. Robb, do you have any comment about the abrupt departure of Ms. Abruzzo from your agency or the facts contained in this article?

Why is your FOIA Officer Synta Keeling being permitted under your leadership to continue to conceal FOIA requests for official government documents and not respond to repeated requests for information from Mr. Edwards (see NLRB FOIA tracking numbers: LR-2017-1152, LR-2017-1264, LR-2017-1283, LR-2017-1297, and LR-2017-1313).

Your public affairs office has been non-responsive. If you care to issue a comment or response please reply in writing by email to Mr. Edwards directly.

Warmest Regards

Capitol Hellway Media Company LLC

A Free Media Company in the 21st Century

No comment was received from Mr. Robb.

CONGRESSIONAL RESPONSE

According to a letter dated January 9, 2018, from Congressman Mario Diaz-Balart, the Department of Justice is now reviewing the conduct of Prem Aburvasamy, Eric Marks and other NLRB officials involved in the complaint.

MARIO DIAZ-BALART

Congress of the United States
House of Representatives
Washington, DC 20515-0925

January 9, 2018

Mr. John S. Edwards

Dear Mr. Edwards:

I am writing to advise you that my district office has received an interim response from the U.S. Department of Justice, which replies to the inquiry made on your behalf. I have enclosed a copy for your review.

Upon receipt of further information about your case, I will contact you again. In the meantime, if you have any questions or receive any news please contact my Senior Congressional Aide, @mail.house.gov.

Sincerely,

Mario Diaz-Balart
Member of Congress

MDB:ya
encl.

From: DOJ Correspondence (SMO)
Sent: Monday, January 08, 2018 2:18 PM
To:
Subject: FW: Congressional Inquiry (Edwards)
Importance: High

Good afternoon

After the review is completed a written response will be sent to Congressman Diaz-Balart. Thank you for your inquiry.

U.S. Department of Justice

It is expected that Aburvasamy and Marks will experience the same fate as Abruzzo or be exterminated from federal workforce in some other way.

Please help fire these parasites!

NOTES

1. See NLRB FOIA Tracking Numbers: LR-2017-1152, LR-2017-1264, LR-2017-1283, LR-2017-1297, and LR-2017-1313.

2. See APPEAL Letter LR-2017-1152 dated April 10, 2017 to NLRB FOIA Supervisor Denise Meiners / Phone: (202) 273-2935 / Email: Denise.Meiners @nlrb.gov and others.

Lafe Solomon – the Scariest Person in Government

Why do we have the Executive Order –Fair Pay and Safe Workplaces?

Did you know that it is being implemented right now in our government by a radical left wing activist at the Department of Labor and no President can stop him? Do you know why they can't stop them? Because the White House is full of bubble heads who haven't got a fucking clue. Doesn't matter which party is in power, bubble heads run our government.

Lafe Solomon is a bubble head. He was considered by Watchdog.org to be one of the Scariest People of 2016. And then Watchdog.org suddenly disappeared. Poof. They were gone. And a few days after this article was published, the Whistleblower who provided background information was fired.

Lafe Solomon was the U.S. Department of Labor senior labor compliance adviser that was in charge of implementing the 2014 "Fair Pay and Safe Workplaces" executive order signed by President Obama on July 31, 2014. He formerly worked at the NLRB, but had a few issues with that.

Supreme Court Holds that Lafe Solomon Improperly Served as NLRB General Counsel

Inside the beltway this order is known as the "Blacklisting Rule."
the order says:

```
"This order seeks to increase efficiency and cost savings in the
work performed by parties who contract with the Federal
Government by ensuring that they understand and comply with
labor laws" and regulations.
```

The effect this executive order has is that it creates purpose and establishes intent for out of control government involvement and corruption. Those businesses that the government favors will be permitted to receive government contracts and as an extension, progressively any state or locality that receives federal funding. This is one of the back-doors that was being built by President Obama and Tom Perez to control businesses – through the control of people through regulations. It is also part of the Democrats electoral strategy to control conservative districts, make them weaker. Tom Perez who is coincidentally in the running to be the next Chair of the Democratic National Committee of course has been written about widely in this blog for widespread discrimination and corruption. Update: Tom

Perez went on to become DNC Chair. He has taken the Democrat Party to Socialism.

The EEOC, NLRB, EPA, Justice Department and other regulatory bodies collect this data now and are using it collaboratively today to build that political blacklisting machine Obama and Perez were to planning to pass to Hillary Clinton. It is still happening.

The next section of the executive order says:

```
"Helping executive departments and agencies (agencies) to
identify and work with contractors with track records of
compliance will reduce execution delays and avoid distractions
and complications that arise from contracting with contractors
with track records of noncompliance."
```

Government "Helping" means a big bureaucracy we don't need and can't afford. This also means the government can say, "If you don't do what I want, you can't get money." If a Democrat is ever in control of the White House again, this is one of the weapons they will utilize.

We need to focus on reducing regulations everywhere now, add back what we need later. Update: Trump did just that and the economy in 2019 is booming.

We need to reverse this executive order – which still has not been done – and end this back-door to power for government bureaucracies.

NLRB CIO Prem Aburvasamy Violates Federal Law

Federal Chief Information Officer **Prem Aburvasamy** and his deputy **Charles Eric Marks** at the National Labor Relations Board, *a.k.a. NLRB*, must be fired, and under no circumstances should they ever be hired for any job as a federal contractor or civil servant for life.

In 2017, the NLRB Inspector General **David Potts Berry** covered up evidence that proves beyond a reasonable doubt that Aburvasamy and Marks swindled more than $10 million of taxpayer money through contract fraud at the NLRB, and then retaliated against the employee who blew the whistle on them.[1]

Inspector General Berry, a Democrat and notorious deep state operative, is also under scrutiny for using a partisan ethics probe to help popular left wing radical politicians in the resistance movement. The purpose of that probe was to smear Republican board members who oversee the agency that were appointed by President Trump.

Aburvasamy, Marks and Berry are examples of scumbags that we can do without in our government and the U.S. Merit Systems Protection Board has everything you need to prove it. Sadly...MSPB decisions will take a while and the backlog is tremendous.

But I digress. Let me be clear – I have no intention of harming anyone. I am speaking metaphorically. I do think, however, that Aburvasamy, Marks and Berry present a clear and present danger to everyone who works with them. Every employer should be very concerned about having these three working together on their payrolls, but that's just my opinion – and your business.

The time has come for a peaceful revolt against corruption at the National Labor Relations Board. I call on all Americans to tell Congress and the President to end the careers of bureaucrats at the NLRB who abused their authority and violated federal laws.

Today's employers of the NLRB *"corruption cartel"* should stand up for justice and whistleblower rights by helping end the careers of these three criminals, and by never allowing them to be hired for a federal government affiliated job. If they apply for a job with you, don't hire them! They are poison in the workplace. We need to show the Shadow Government that sunshine is coming and soon they will be disinfected.

NOTES

1. See U.S. Merit Systems Protection Board docket number DC-0752-17-0467-I-1 / John S. Edwards v. National Labor Relations Board / for case documents and material evidence to substantiate all allegations against named individuals in this article.

Prem Aburvasamy Must be Fired

Chief Information Officer **Prem Aburvasamy** and his co-conspirators at the National Labor Relations Board, *a.k.a. NLRB*, must be fired.

The purpose of this article is to draw public attention to Six Corrupt U.S. Government officials who need to be fired. There are many, many more where all the scumbags work – the corrupt NLRB.

At the NLRB, I exposed more than $10 million in wasteful spending, contract fraud and many other violations of the law by Chief Information Officer **Prem Aburvasamy** and his co-conspirators Inspector General **David Potts Berry,** attorney **Elizabeth Bach,** FOIA officer **Synta Keeling,** Executive Secretary **Roxanne Rothschild** and **Eric Marks.**[1]

I think government parasites are the most despicable and horrible things on earth. They are viruses, diseases, and I am absolutely convinced that one day all **Whistleblower Retaliators** will be eradicated from society in a vengeful and tortuous manner.

As reported earlier, **Philip Miscimarra** and his sidekick **Jennifer Abruzzo** have already been terminated from the federal government for their roles in corruption, contract fraud and discriminating against a disabled Veteran. Miscimarra returned to his old job and Abruzzo is working her way down the union lawyer ladder.

However, the means to cover-up crimes and retaliate against Whistleblowers at the NLRB is still being paid for by taxpayers. This spending is counter-productive and must be terminated with extreme prejudice.

The entire scheme to retaliate against me was concocted by attorney **Elizabeth Bach** who is still burrowed inside the agency and paid by taxpayers.

ELIZABETH BACH
ATTORNEY, NLRB

Elizabeth Bach is the taxpayer funded NLRB attorney who defends corrupt government officials with control over a $270 million taxpayer funded budget. It's backwards. Whistleblowers have to pay to defend themselves out of their personal savings or by selling their homes. Elizabeth Bach should be defending my rights and not defending criminals.

I was fortunate. I won my lawsuit after spending a few bills, but most people who get fired the way I did don't come back alive. My investigation required that I blow the whistle. Their response is what I have reported.

Elizabeth Bach, Synta Keeling and David Potts Berry are partisan political bureaucrats who present a clear and present danger to the U.S. federal government because they retaliate against Whistleblowers. Prem Aburvasamy is an immoral piece of shit who should be scraped from the shoe of

American citizenship and shipped back to India where he currently sells American jobs and immigrant work visas illegally to hundreds of students for a fee.

If their government bosses won't take action to terminate these Whistle-blower Retaliators...

Perhaps someday – someone will.

NOTES

1. See U.S. Merit Systems Protection Board docket number DC-0752-17-0467-I-1 / John S. Edwards v. National Labor Relations Board / for case documents and material evidence to substantiate all allegations against named individuals in this article

Killing Prem Aburvasamy and Eric Marks

On December 6, 2017, a DHS agent and Sheriff's counterintelligence officer showed up at 9 a.m. on the doorstep of my residence in southwest Florida without any warning – not even a phone call – and coincidentally just six days after I first published my story about corruption at the NLRB.

Prem Aburvasamy and Eric Marks are corrupt government bureaucrats who work together at the National Labor Relations Board (NLRB) in Washington, D.C. I used to work for them. On November 30, 2017, I published the story, *"Killing Whistleblower Retaliators at the NLRB"* that exposed corruption at the $275 million per year taxpayer funded government agency.

At the conclusion of the interrogation, the agents told my wife and me that we should "be careful" and contact them directly if we see anything unusual like our "cats getting killed" or sudden vandalism at our home. They said that they were just, "doing what some SES in Washington ordered," and acknowledged that it was Prem Aburvasamy, the Chief Information Officer at the NLRB and his deputy Eric Marks, who ordered the intimidation.

I requested and was granted permission to record some of the interrogation. The counterintelligence officer would not speak unless the recorder was off, which I obliged. Each agent was provided a copy of this article. The two agents asked and I agreed to not publish the audio recording or reveal their identities. They said that they fear retaliation if I publish their names together with the details of our conversation and because they don't want to be seen as co-conspirators for the corruption I exposed at the NLRB. The two agents behaved like good men who were just following ridiculous orders from parasitic bureaucrats in Washington D.C.[1] They knew what I knew. If they blew the whistle, nothing would be done and they would be fired.

One of the interrogators even issued a congratulatory, "Keep up the great work" and "expose the bastards!" after he acknowledged the abuse of power he was participating in.

The DHS case number to substantiate this article is N17003708.[2] Also see DHS FOIA Request Number 2018-NPFO-000152 to substantiate these facts.

Here is the response to my Freedom of Information Act requests from the NLRB Office of Inspector General dated February 21, 2019.[3]

United States Government

NATIONAL LABOR RELATIONS BOARD

OFFICE OF INSPECTOR GENERAL

Washington, DC 20570-0001

February 21, 2019

This letter is in response to your Freedom of Information Act requests:

The OIG neither admits nor denies the existence of the information you seek because any such confirmation or denial would harm the interests of the NLRB.

Sincerely,

James E. Tatum, Jr.
Counsel to the Inspector General

The Interrogation

To dispatch agents to our home, Prem Aburvasamy and Eric Marks alleged that they fear for their lives because of a story I published. In the complaint, Prem Aburvasamy alleged that I was going to kill him.

CORRUPT GOVERNMENT OFFICIALS

Prem Aburvasamy
CHIEF INFORMATION
OFFICER

Eric Marks
LONG-TENURED
BUREAUCRAT

On November 30, 2017, I published the story, "Killing Whistleblower Retaliators at the NLRB" using satirical art in which I described the retaliation that my family suffered at the hands of Aburvasamy, Marks and other corrupt federal government employees in Washington D.C.

In the article, I wrote that, *"I believe that [Aburvasamy and Marks] have committed and covered up crimes against the United States of America and should be fired, publicly humiliated and never allowed to work again in any job paid for by taxpayers for the rest of their lives."*

I also explained that, *"Working at the NLRB was surreal. At times, I imagined that I was working for the mafia. The NLRB has two classes of employees who work there. The workers who are too afraid to blow the whistle, and the executives who are too corrupt to be held accountable."*[4]

For the record, I do not intend to murder Washington swamp creatures Aburvasamy and Marks.

I hope to help inform the public and Congress about their poor character and corruption so that President Trump's new General Counsel will take action to kill their jobs and #draintheswamp in Washington D.C.

As the law enforcement officers left our home, we recognized the absurdity of the complaint and its purpose. A Senior Special Agent for DHS had to drive many hours from a distant city just to knock on our door to investigate an absurd charge. This latest act of retaliation by Aburvasamy and Marks is just another example of the two conspiring to make ridiculous complaints against a Whistleblower, and then use the investigative resources of a federal government agency to carry it out.

It also proves the power and reach that corrupt federal government employees like Aburvasamy, Marks and their bosses have been provided at taxpayer expense to intimidate federal government employees who blow the whistle, leave the federal government and move far away.

Justice

In my opinion, Prem Aburvasamy is a corrupt and dangerous federal government employee who needs to be terminated now. Charles Eric Marks is Aburvasamy's deputy and should be fired for his scandalous participation and breaking the law. Peter B. Robb[5] is their new supervisor who started work at the NLRB on November 17, 2017, after being appointed by President Trump. And, Robb's deputy is still Jennifer Abruzzo who I think should be fired too.

UPDATE!

On Friday December 29, 2017 – Jennifer Abruzzo was fired!!!

PETER B. ROBB
GENERAL COUNSEL NLRB

The whistleblower retaliation story I published was not the only reason that federal law enforcement visited my home to interrogate me. President Trump's new appointee was involved too.

On December 3, 2017, I emailed NLRB General Counsel Peter B. Robb and offered him congratulations on his new job along with a *link to my story.* **I also wrote,** *"Your current deputy, Jennifer Abruzzo, was serving a noncareer appointment prior to your arrival there. Sources inside your agency tell me that before your confirmation, Abruzzo was planning to remain at the agency – either as your deputy, or in a career SES position that she created prior to your appointment. As the article explains, I am publishing an investigative series about the corruption that I witnessed at the agency by Abruzzo and her* *retaliation against me for blowing the whistle. Whether you keep her or not, I would love the opportunity to interview you about your decision before I publish the next article about corruption and whistleblower retaliation at your agency.* **The focus of that article is either going to be Abruzzo's retention by you, or her dismissal/departure.**"

UPDATE!

On Friday December 29, 2017 – Jennifer Abruzzo was fired!!!

I followed up with Mr. Robb and the NLRB Public Affairs Office for comment two days later on December 5, 2017, and discovered that my emails to Mr. Robb and Public Affairs were being monitored and blocked by the NLRB CIO [Aburvasamy] and could not be delivered. Using another email account that I verified with Robb earlier, we were able to email this message to him on December 5th and confirm delivery.

"Mr Robb, your CIO has taken actions to block our emails to you, and to your Public Affairs Office seeking comment (on my article). Did Aburvasamy do this at your direction? Does this mean that you are going to retain Abruzzo in the agency and join the technology corruption cartel that has existed there for decades? Let us know how best to contact your agency."

And the next day, on December 6, 2017, I was ambushed by law enforcement at my home to threaten and intimidate my family.

There is clearly a causal link between communicating corruption to NLRB government employees and swift retaliation by them using taxpayer funded investigative services to carry it out. One year ago, it was the Inspector General David Potts Berry who concocted an investigation for Aburvasamy and Marks when I worked for the government and blew the whistle on them. Now, they are using the same playbook with the Department of Homeland Security because I am a civilian now and outside the reach of their corrupt $275 million per year taxpayer budget.

THE BOTTOM LINE

On Wednesday December 6, 2017, the NLRB corruption cartel dispatched a DHS Senior Special Agent and a counterintelligence officer to interrogate me and my wife without Miranda inside our home. The surprise interrogation took place after I published this article on November 30, 2017.

Aburvasamy and Marks have been permitted by their bosses to intimidate my family and threaten me using government resources paid for by taxpayers.

IMPORTANT ARTIFACTS

At 7:30 PM on December 6, 2017 the following email message was delivered to the NLRB General Counsel Peter Robb:

To: peter.robb@nlrb.gov

Mr. Robb, I was visited by federal law enforcement today. I hope you will read my latest article about that. I see you are continuing to block my emails and have no intention of responding to my requests for an interview or comment.

Please direct your staff to stop harassing me. My wife and I feel threatened and fear for our lives. If the threats and retaliation continue, I will report you to the appropriate authorities and post my complaints online. I am a journalist and you don't have to respond to my requests for information. But the law (5 U.S.C. § 552) does require that you respond to my FOIA requests which your agency still has not done. And I have rights under the U.S. Constitution that you may be attempting to deny.[6]

John Stuart Edwards / Journalist

On December 11, 2017, an official complaint was filed by Congressman Mario Diaz-Balart (R-FL) with the *U.S. Department of Justice* to investigate National Labor Relations Board General Counsel Peter B. Robb, Jennifer Abruzzo, Prem Aburvasamy and Charles Eric Marks for abuse of authority and for violating an investigative journalist's Constitutional Rights.

Three weeks later, Abruzzo abruptly resigned.

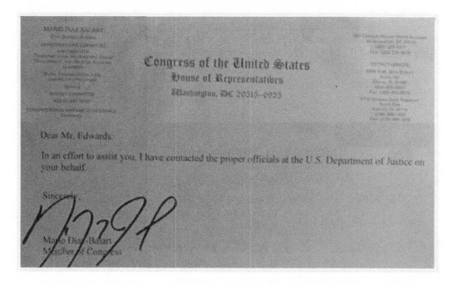

According to a letter dated January 9, 2018, from Congressman Mario Diaz-Balart, the Department of Justice is reviewing the conduct of Prem Aburvasamy, Eric Marks and other NLRB officials involved in the complaint. Aburvasamy and Marks must face justice.

Many Freedom of Information Act -FOIA requests have been made.

On February 10, 2019, an official complaint was filed with Congressman Mario Diaz-Balart (R-FL) to request access to many FOIA requests made to the NLRB.

The following response to this story was received from the NLRB Office of Inspector General on February 21, 2019:

United States Government

NATIONAL LABOR RELATIONS BOARD

OFFICE OF INSPECTOR GENERAL

Washington, DC 20570-0001

February 21, 2019

This letter is in response to your Freedom of Information Act requests:

The OIG neither admits nor denies the existence of the information you seek because any such confirmation or denial would harm the interests of the NLRB.

Sincerely,

James E. Tatum, Jr.
Counsel to the Inspector General

The following email was sent to the NLRB Office of Inspector General on February 21, 2019 after the above response was received:

From: John Stuart Edwards

To: james.tatum@nlrb.gov

Cc: Synta.Keeling@nlrb.gov

Sent: Thu, Feb 21, 2019 1:30 pm

Subject: re: FOIA response letter

Mr. Tatum,

Thank you for your prompt response confirming the corruption cover-up at the NLRB. We have obtained the unredacted reports identified as those requested under the FOIA from sources inside the government with access to the information. Since the OIG neither admits nor denies the existence of the information, those unredacted reports will be published at the appropriate time along with your responses to inform the public and to substantiate additional charges against personnel at your agency.

If you care to comment on any story involving the corruption and cover-up by the OIG and FOIA Officer at the NLRB, please send your responses to the email below.

Thank you,
John Stuart Edwards
Capitol Hellway Media Company LLC
capitolhellway@gmail.com

As of Tuesday April 23, 2019, no action has been taken by Congressman Mario Diaz-Balart to address the absence of action by the Justice Department into the allegations about National Labor Relations Board that I officially made to him on December 11, 2017.

As of Tuesday April 23, 2019, no action has been taken by Congressman Mario Diaz-Balart (R-FL) to address my FOIA requests.

NOTES

1. See DHS FOIA Request Number 2018-NPFO-000152 to substantiate these facts.

2. The DHS Senior Special Agent and the law enforcement officer who visited our home on December 6, 2017 were professional and courteous at all times when they spoke with us and they did not make any specific verbal threats to commit murder and end our lives.

3. See the article FOIA CORRUPTION – by SYNTA KEELING at the NLRB for details about my FOIA requests.

4. See "Obama pick for NLRB was top lawyer for union tainted by mob ties, history of corruption"

5. Peter B. Robb (born 01/24/1948) and wife Kathleen K. Robb (born 06/07/1949) – reside at 141 Piney Brook Way, Brattleboro, Vermont; and Sutton Place, Longboat Key, Florida.

6. See NLRB FOIA tracking numbers: LR-2017-1152, LR-2017-1264, LR-2017-1283, LR-2017-1297, and LR-2017-1313.

Killing Whistleblower Retaliators at the NLRB

This article explains why **Phillip Miscimarra** departed the federal government at the end of his term as the **Chairman of the National Labor Relations Board** on December 16, 2017, despite being asked by President Trump to serve another term.

> "Metaphorically, if the victims of sexual assault are whistleblowers, then I was gang-raped by **Phillip Miscimarra**," said John Stuart Edwards, a Whistleblower for the National Labor Relations Board. "It disgusts me that this piece of shit – Miscimarra – presided over U.S. labor law disputes impacting millions of workers across the country while he was retaliating against me. He should have been fired sooner!"

THE STORY "HOW PHILLIP MISCIMARRA RAPED ME"

I am a retired *United States Marine Corps Mustang*. That means I enlisted in the Marines before becoming an officer. I am also a professional killer. After I left the military, I worked for small companies and large corporations where I achieved a comfortable level of prosperity. I built a reputation for being an honest, results-driven leader with high skills in software development and continuous improvement.

After learning that the U.S. federal government was planning to waste more than ***one trillion dollars*** of taxpayer money during the next decade on technology spending, I decided to leave the "sanity" of the private sector in order to serve my country again in the federal government. I believed that I could help create a government that is more secure, works better and costs a fraction of what it costs today to operate. I even created a promotional YouTube video to explain my call to public service. I was told that this video helped me get hired for my first government job at *Homeland Security* to modernize the national E-Verify system.[1]

WASHINGTON IS A DEADLY SWAMP!

During my short career working at the Washington D.C. headquarters of the National Labor Relations Board, *a.k.a. NLRB*, I exposed more than $10 million in wasteful spending by the technology department. I uncovered extensive contract fraud by long-tenured federal government bureaucrats. And I witnessed the falsification and tampering with official government records by senior officials including the NLRB Inspector General David Potts Berry and FOIA Officer Synta Keeling.

Working at the NLRB was surreal. At times, I imagined that I was working for the mafia. The NLRB has two classes of employees who work there. The workers who are too afraid to blow the whistle, and the executives who are too corrupt to be held accountable.[2]

WHISTLEBLOWER RETALIATION

Anyone who stands up against corrupt federal government bureaucrats will be obliterated.

After blowing the whistle on Prem Aburvasamy and Eric Marks, I was threatened and harassed. In a meeting about my complaints, Eric Marks told me that "military veterans and their styles of leadership are not welcome at the NLRB" and "directness and honesty at this agency is not part of the culture." Marks knew that I was hired by the agency under the veteran's preference program as a disabled veteran.

Eric Marks has worked in the NLRB technology department as a contractor or federal employee for more than two decades. In my opinion, Marks has the technology skills and leadership ability of an admin clerk who should be paid a salary of about thirty thousand dollars. Marks gets paid $162,000 per year plus federal benefits by the NLRB, and he has been paid over $2 million in compensation from U.S. taxpayers during his tenure there.

Aburvasamy joined the NLRB in 2014 as deputy CIO, and was promoted to the CIO position and Senior Executive Service by Chairman Miscimarra in May 2016.

On November 30, 2016, I made a written protected whistleblower complaint to the General Counsel, the Inspector General David Potts Berry and the entire Board at the NLRB, including the current Chairman Philip A. Miscimarra. In an email with the subject *"Request for Help,"* I complained that my current working environment was hostile. I literally "begged" them to halt the active retaliation that was being carried out against me by Aburvasamy and Marks for making protected whistleblower complaints.

From: Edwards, John
Sent: Wednesday, November 30, 2016 9:03 AM
To: Pearce, Mark G. <Mark.Pearce@nlrb.gov>; Miscimarra, Philip A. <Philip.Miscimarra@nlrb.gov>; McFerran, Lauren <Lauren.McFerran@nlrb.gov>; Griffin, Richard F. <Richard.Griffin@nlrb.gov>
Subject: Request for Help

Good morning. My apologies for the intrusion but I have nowhere else to turn. I am your ACIO for Mission Systems which includes NxGen, JCMS and FTS, along with all your scanners and the reporting data warehouse. I joined the NLRB in April 2016 and have quietly done my very best to analyze, stabilize and improve your systems at a lower cost and have produced significant results in a very short time. I supervise 5 bargaining unit employees, and 4 GS14's along with about 10-12 contractors at this time and have made great strides to improving both productivity and morale.

There is a very severe management issue that is spiraling out of control in the OCIO that I feel requires very senior leadership intervention to resolve to protect the reputation of the NLRB and everyone involved. I respectfully request your assistance in resolving the matter internally and appropriately.

I think the attached communications explain the current situation well, which is deteriorating quickly into a hostile work environment for me and making me ill. I beg you to please ask my supervisor Eric Marks and the OCIO Prem Aburvasamy to halt their active retaliation of me until a proper independent investigation into the totality and validity of all the complaints involved can be done.

The next day, on December 1, 2016, the NLRB Inspector General David Potts Berry launched an investigation against me, not my complaints. My co-workers, peers and some of my employees were interviewed. The entire investigation was sloppy and a farce. On December 19, 2016, I met with the Inspector General David Potts Berry who told me, "I don't do investigations when there is no wrongdoing involved which is the case here," referring to his investigation of me. This is substantiated by the fact that on January 3, 2017, NLRB Inspector General David Potts Berry issued a memorandum stating that he did not substantiate any of the false allegations made against me – including those that I ended up being fired for that are described below.

> None of my whistleblower complaints have ever been investigated by the NLRB Inspector General David Potts Berry or anyone else who works in the federal government.

In early February 2017, I was physically removed from my job, placed on administrative leave at home, and then I was fired in an email I received from Aburvasamy that he sent like a coward to my personal email address at 5 p.m. on April 4, 2017. My termination from federal employment was effective immediately.

> According to the termination letter attached to the email, I was being fired by the federal government for two reasons.

First, it was alleged that I violated the leave policy by initially denying a leave request for an employee named Hari Sharma before I approved it.

My response to this charge stated, "According to the NLRB leave and attendance policy PER-10 pg. 16, management has the primary responsibility for determining when and the extent to which annual leave is to be granted. I denied Sharma's leave so that I could check on his well-being, and I approved the leave he requested after I spoke with him."

Federal employee Hari Sharma had submitted a leave request to me after working hours at about 10 p.m. in early November 2016, for the following day. I denied his request using an online leave request system at about

11 p.m. Early the next morning, I called Sharma at home and asked if he was OK. Sharma said that he had contractors working at his home and so I suggested that he telework for a few hours so that he could dial into a meeting that I wanted him to attend. He said he didn't want to attend the meeting, so I approved his leave.

In his termination letter firing me, Aburvasamy stated that he was sustaining this charge because he said "this conduct was improper and inappropriate." Sharma and Aburvasamy both immigrated to the United States from India and are close friends.

In the second charge, it was alleged that during mid-year performance reviews in January 2016, for NLRB federal employees Ying Xing and Hari Sharma, I told them that I would keep their ratings confidential and not share my feedback about their performance with other employees.

My response to this charge explained in detail my method for conducting performance reviews and stated, "This charge is ridiculous."

In his termination letter, Aburvasamy wrote that he was sustaining the charge because "this practice flies in the face of the efficient functioning of the federal service and there is no rational basis for you to tell employees that you will keep their ratings confidential."[3]

Miscimarra, Abruzzo, Rothschild, Aburvasamy and Marks wanted me out of the agency because I was the only employee who worked there that took steps to curtail the wasteful spending that had plagued the organization for many years. I did this by re-structuring a contract that was going to be awarded in March 2017. The new contract would have significantly reduced licensing, maintenance and labor costs for taxpayers, and that is not what they wanted to happen.

JENNIFER A. ABRUZZO
DEPUTY GENERAL COUNSEL NLRB

The NLRB is a small government agency with about 1,600 employees and obviously it was no secret that I had blown the whistle loud and clear.

During a meeting in October 2016, an Assistant General Counsel named Elizabeth Kilpatrick warned me that her boss, long tenured NLRB bureaucrat Deputy General Counsel Jennifer Abruzzo, had a long history at the agency of covering up corruption. She said, "Jennifer feels that the changes you are implementing to remove waste, fraud and abuse will reflect poorly on her past performance." In other words, Kilpatrick was sent as an envoy to tell me that Abruzzo – a government attorney and career bureaucrat, did not want to be held accountable for wasting taxpayer money and allowing contract fraud. In my dealings with Abruzzo, I found her to be a liberal narcissist who put herself above others and acted very irrational at times.

Peter B. Robb[4] was appointed by President Trump and sworn in as General Counsel of the National Labor Relations Board on November 17, 2017 for a four year term. If Abruzzo remains at the NLRB under Robb, that should be a clear signal to the world that the corruption cartel that is embedded at the NLRB will continue to be protected and allowed to work there.

Another Abruzzo comrade at the agency who played a major role in my retaliation was NLRB Deputy Executive Secretary Roxanne Rothschild. Rothschild and her husband, Bryan Burnett, together managed the team that was in charge of the NLRB's technology investment portfolio from 2006 through December 2015. This Washington D.C. power couple managed about $16 million per year on average in taxpayer spending for technology. That comes to approximately $10,000 per employee each year for a phone, laptop computer, software applications and internet connection. And the quality of the products they purchased and implemented totally sucked. It was not hard for me or any rational outsider with business IT experience to see that there was something dreadfully wrong with the technology spending at the NLRB that Marks and Aburvasamy wanted covered up.

In addition to the wasteful spending they carried out during Burnett's time at the agency, another reason Rothschild took actions to have me fired was to protect her husband from being prosecuted for his poor stewardship of taxpayer money. Burnett had left the NLRB and took a job, coincidentally, as the CIO of the Equal Employment Opportunity Commission where claims of discrimination are reported. Insiders at that agency who work for him told me that his performance has been lackluster at best. Burnett and his wife are clearly swamp creatures who make a living feeding off government largesse in Washington D.C.

Rothschild gets paid $162,000 per year and Burnett is paid $170,000. Together, they rake in over $332,000 per year plus federal benefits, and have been paid over $10 million in compensation from U.S. taxpayers during their tenures.

THE CORRUPTION STARTS AT THE TOP

To instill fear of retaliation across the entire organization and continue the culture of corruption there, NLRB Chairman Phillip Miscimarra ordered what amounted to a public lynching of me, and then he directly supervised each and every step of the retaliation carried out against me by his executive team.

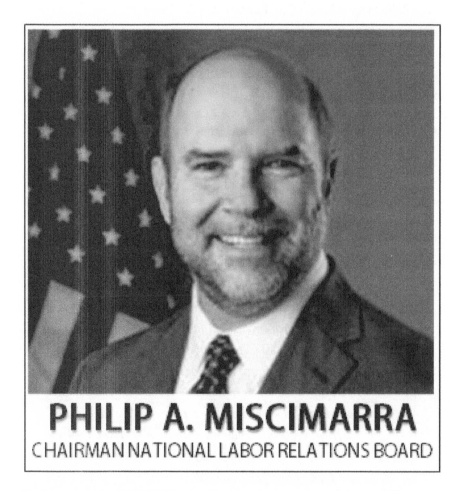

PHILIP A. MISCIMARRA
CHAIRMAN NATIONAL LABOR RELATIONS BOARD

On January 23, 2017, Philip A. Miscimarra was named Acting Chairman of the NLRB by President Trump. Just two weeks after his appointment, I was escorted out of the building by an armed uniformed security guard like a criminal. Senior executives, my peers, junior staff and contractors were all gathered while I was still in my office in order to watch my departure. They formed a gauntlet of shame in the hallway to watch. This blatant public display of retaliation was planned and cruelly carried out by Prem Aburvasamy and Eric Marks to defame my character and diminish my credibility as a witness against them. This final act of public humiliation sent a clear message to the entire workforce that if you blow the whistle, you will be targeted and assassinated from your job.[5]

During my administrative leave, I remained in constant email contact with Miscimarra. Each time I informed Miscimarra of violations of the law and retaliation by his staff, which he acknowledged, the retaliation intensified.

Here are some quotes from an email that provides some context for my communications with Chairman Miscimarra.

"Chairman, I requested your help in an email to you dated Wednesday, November 30, 2016 at 9:03 AM. Two days later, on Friday, December 02, 2016, at the direction of (Abruzzo) and (Aburvasamy and Marks), NLRB Special Counsel Elizabeth Bach told me that "former military personnel are not a good fit at the NLRB" and that "certain adverse action" will be carried out against me by the agency for notifying you of my concerns. Ms. Bach carried out her threat against me within days after you were appointed Chairman by the President of the United States. The retaliation she (and the Inspector General David Potts Berry) ordered against me was formulated in secret with Deputy CIO Eric Marks and is fully documented and explained in the attachments to this email. In 25 years of exemplary military and civilian federal service, I have never seen retaliation to destroy a distinguished veteran's career, reputation and family's financial security so deceptively and cruelly carried out in full view of an organization's senior leaders and junior staff. I served in the Marines for two decades, and in that organization which is the best in the world, my Generals cared more

about accomplishing the mission and the welfare of their troops than
their powerful positions. That is the hallmark of real leadership in
public service. These people who work for you have obviously never
been held accountable in the past, so I guess there is no reason for them
to expect that they will be held accountable by you now."

CORRUPT AND INCOMPETENT MANAGEMENT

The NLRB is an independent U.S. federal government agency with responsibilities for enforcing U.S. labor law. I was hired in April 2016, as Associate
CIO to fix a portfolio of failing software applications that suffered for many
years because of the incompetent management and corrupt practices of
Abruzzo, Rothschild, Burnett, Aburvasamy and Marks.

In just two months, I had implemented many solutions to the problems
that had plagued the agency for many years. I was modernizing software
applications and migrating software from high cost on premise hosting
to more economical commercial cloud hosting. At the time of my firing,
key metrics were already showing results that included reduced system
down time and increased access to applications by mobile devices. Also,
many new application features for customers were being delivered without
any increased costs. Productivity by my federal staff and contractors had
more than quadrupled, and mission application users were delighted by the
changes we made and the projects we had undertaken.

At great personal expense, I hired an attorney and provided comprehensive material evidence to the Merit Systems Protection Board judge. I was
easily able to prove beyond a reasonable doubt that senior NLRB officials
made false official statements and conspired to fabricate frivolous charges
against me in retaliation for blowing the whistle.

Chairman Miscimarra, Inspector General David Potts Berry, Deputy Gen-
eral Counsel Jennifer Abruzzo, Special Counsel Elizabeth Bach, Roxanne
Rothschild, Bryan Burnett, Prem Aburvasamy, Eric Marks, FOIA Officer
Synta Keeling, and employees Hari Sharma and Ying Xing were all named

as co-conspirators in my lawsuit filed with the MSPB on April 25, 2017.

I believe that all these people have committed and covered up crimes against the United States of America and should be fired, publicly humiliated and never allowed to work again in any job paid for by taxpayers for the rest of their lives.

THE SETTLEMENT

Despite being ambushed and tossed from the building, I managed to obtain copies of all the reports, documents, and emails that I needed to prove my case in court from sources at the NLRB. I also made recordings of some key meetings that support everything you have read in this article, and I made several Freedom of Information Act requests that FOIA Officer Synta Keeling has ignored.[6]

At the time of publication for this article, none of my FOIA requests have been legally fulfilled. In her latest email update to me dated October 19, 2017, Synta Keeling said she was still processing my requests made earlier this year.

After I filed my lawsuit with the Merit Systems Protection Board, Miscimarra quickly settled with me and met all my demands in order to avoid accountability and publicity. I told Miscimarra that there was no way on earth that I could ever return to an agency that is so evil and corrupt. Everything that I asked for in my first settlement offer, Miscimarra agreed to without a counter offer. I was awarded a settlement by the NLRB that was ratified on May 18, 2017. I was reinstated as a federal employee, paid back pay and leave, and reimbursed for all my legal expenses. I resigned from the agency on June 6, 2017 with exactly five years and one month federal service. Miscimarra considered it a win because he did not want this case to go to court. And I agreed in the settlement to not file another complaint against the NLRB in exchange for me being allowed to publish my story.

MISCIMARRA'S LEGACY

"I heard the sound of You in the garden, and I was afraid because I was naked; so I hid myself" (New American Standard Bible, Genesis 3:10)."

On August 9, 2017, it was reported that Miscimarra would not seek reappointment to the Board for family reasons despite being encouraged by the Trump administration to do so. Coincidentally, that same day I received a phone call from an attorney who works in the NLRB Inspector General's office who said that he was interested in investigating Aburvasamy for concealing official government records.

About an hour later, I received a call from the NLRB Inspector General David Potts Berry and he told me that he was finally going to investigate the allegations that I had made that caused me to be fired. I told David Potts Berry that under the settlement, "I agreed to not file any additional cases, claims, grievances, or complaints regarding my employment with the Agency, except regarding enforcement of the settlement should I believe the Agency has not fulfilled its obligations."

The next day, I received the following email from Elizabeth Bach stating that I could speak with the Inspector General David Potts Berry.

-----Original Message-----
From: Bach, Elizabeth H. <Elizabeth.Bach@nlrb.gov>
To: John Stuart Edwards
Sent: Thu, Aug 10, 2017 10:17 am
Subject: Ability to cooperate with the Agency Inspector General

Dear Mr. Edwards,

I hope this email finds you in good health.

At the behest of the Inspector General, I just want to assure you that the settlement agreement reached between you and the Agency does not prevent you from cooperating with any investigatory process by the IG.

Please feel free to contact me should you have questions or concerns.

Very truly yours,

Elizabeth H. Bach
Special Counsel
National Labor Relations Board

After receiving this email from Bach, I never heard back from the Inspector General's office or anyone at the NLRB about an investigation into my complaints.

There is a long history at the NLRB of Prem Aburvasamy hiring ethnic friends and there have been complaints made against him at the agency that Inspector General David Potts Berry has refused to investigate.

Note: this image was removed from the NLRB IG website after first being reported in this story

Submission #187

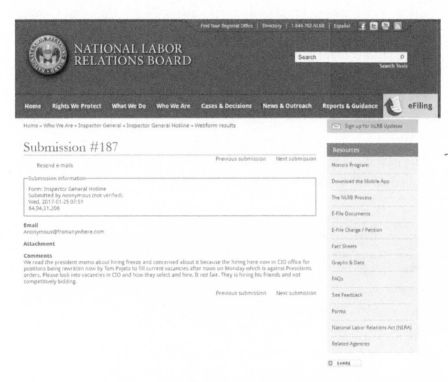

In late August, I contacted some of my sources inside the NLRB. They told me that my predecessor, who had left the NLRB for a higher paying job at the U.S. Patent Office, mysteriously returned to the NLRB for much lesser pay – ostensibly so that he could help Aburvasamy, Marks and Berry continue to cover-up the matter. Sivaram Ghorakavi was rehired by the

NLRB and he is paid $162,000 per year plus federal benefits. Based on the disastrous state of the organization that I inherited from this guy when I arrived there, I'd characterize him as a loser with all caps. Ghorakavi is from India of course, and just like his buddy Sharma, is close friends with Aburvasamy.

Note: this image was removed from the NLRB IG website after first being reported in this story.

Submission #197

This article explains why Phillip Miscimarra, who was appointed by President Obama departed the federal government at the end of his term as the Chairman of the National Labor Relations Board on December 16, 2017, despite being asked by President Trump to serve another term.

If the victims of sexual assault are whistleblowers, then I was gang-raped by Phillip Miscimarra. Please share my story. Help expose Whistleblower Retaliation @NLRB

NOTES

1. The 2011 video called "HOW TO CUT DEFENSE SPENDING RIGHT NOW" explains how to modernize legacy information systems and reduce federal technology costs by simplifying government processes and reusing DoD solutions in civilian U.S. federal agencies. E-Verify is an Internet-based system that compares information from an employee's Employment Eligibility Verification Form I-9 to data from the U.S. Department of Homeland Security and Social Security Administration to confirm employment eligibility.

2. See "Obama pick for NLRB was top lawyer for union tainted by mob ties, history of corruption"

3. See U.S. Merit Systems Protection Board docket number DC-0752-17-0467-I-1 / John S. Edwards v. National Labor Relations Board / for case documents and material evidence to substantiate all allegations against named individuals in this article.

4. Peter B. Robb (born 01/24/1948) and wife Kathleen K. Robb (born 06/07/1949) – reside at 141 Piney Brook Way, Brattleboro, Vermont; and Sutton Place, Longboat Key, Florida.

5. See request ID: LR-2017-1264 / made under the Freedom of Information Act (FOIA), 5 U.S.C. § 552, dated March 25, 2017 and received by NLRB FOIA Officer Synta Keeling on March 27, 2017 / to corroborate the request for the names, position titles, grades, email address and phone numbers for all staff employed by the NLRB on February 7, 2017, and contractors and visitors who were present in the headquarters office located at 1015 Half Street, S.E. 3rd Floor, Washington, D.C. at any time during that day. As of November 30, 2017, no response has been received for this FOIA request from the NLRB FOIA Branch. Also see note 3 for corroboration.

6. See NLRB FOIA tracking numbers: LR-2017-1152, LR-2017-1264, LR-2017-1283, LR-2017-1297, and LR-2017-1313.

The Kavanaugh Paradox

"Judge not from a new standard that we can never understand. Truth and forgiveness must walk hand in hand. For a free society to survive, tolerance must be a virtue, not a demand."

John Stuart Edwards

Streak – to run naked in a public place so as to shock or amuse others.

Moon – to expose one's buttocks in order to insult or amuse someone.

Skinny-Dip – to swim naked in a group.

When I was in high school, these three acts were celebrated and fun – FOR BOTH SEXES – not hostile and offensive like they are today. But then again, back in those days we only had two sexes in the world and very few media snowflakes in this country.

The Kavanaugh Paradox is what happens when a nation is too fragile to heal from its past to follow the rule of law. History may show the Kavanaugh Paradox as the beginning of our demise.

Men, women and all the "other genders" and species and sub-species of humans that the **freaks in the Democrat party** created in the early 21st century must one day be taught to accept history and learn from it; not be conditioned like lab rats as they are now by corrupt mainstream media elites with propaganda machines who dupe their feeble minds into believing that the people who participated in our history and their heirs must be punished and silenced or killed.

The compulsive need by the **freaks in the Democrat party** to destroy historical monuments was the first sign of group clinical psychotic behavior on a large scale. The Kavanaugh confirmation hearings and the Mueller investigation both used *Manchurian Accusers* to further fuel the dangerous psychosis brewing in the Democrat mind. By 2020, the Democrat party was a freak show full of malcontents and losers of every stripe who gave every indication publicly that they had lost their minds.

It is a very sad commentary on the state of education and intelligence in America, but this tragedy is still very dangerous to the world nonetheless.

The United States of America has entered a period of **maximum stupidity.** If it persists, this century will become known as the **Dark Ages for Wisdom** – a period of tremendous power transformation around the globe that resulted from freedom languishing in a polluted sea of fake news and a mob that is enamored by corrupt government officials on social media who want to take away everyone else's rights.

The greatest fear of the American people should not be what has already happened in its history – but what will happen now.

In the early 21st century when the **freaks in the Democrat party** created a culture that made sexuality offensive and denied that life begins in the womb, the people needed to remember that wisdom is the cure for ignorance. Not fighting with each other and not restricting rights.

Wisdom is what they needed. History will show whether they ever found wisdom in time.

Who is Christine Blasey Ford?

Christine Blasey Ford was the first *Manchurian Accuser* to be exposed in public during a U.S. Senate confirmation hearing in 2018.

The **Manchurian Accuser** project was an early 21st century **Central Intelligence Agency** (CIA) mind control experiment used by the **Democrat party** in the United States of America to usurp power by using CIA assets on U.S. soil to infiltrate and sabotage the U.S. government as witnesses against political enemies. It is fascinating how the government uniformly conceals this information from the public.

The Democrat party created a culture that made sexuality offensive and denied that life begins in the womb. Men, women and all the "other genders" and species and sub-species of humans that the **freaks in the Democrat party** created unified against rational policies and took violent actions to deny other Americans their constitutional rights.

Read the Analysis of Christine Blasey Ford's Allegations to fully understand the depths of Democrat party deception and criminality.

According to Ford's Former Boyfriend, "I witnessed Dr. Ford help Monica L. McLean prepare for a potential polygraph exam. Dr. Ford explained in detail what to expect, how polygraphs worked and helped McLean become familiar and less nervous about the exam. Dr. Ford was able to help because of her background in psychology."

THE BATTLE OF THE CENTURY

Christine Blasey Ford
"The First Manchurian Accuser To Be Exposed" VS

Rachel Mitchell
Nominations Investigative Counsel
United States Senate Committee on the Judiciary

Watch Judge Brett Kavanaugh's Response – Under Oath

Throughout the early 21st century, Democrats continued to deploy *Manchurian Accusers* like the ones they used to attack **Supreme Court Justice Brett Kavanaugh** and **President Donald J. Trump** with false allegations and lies. This period became known by some historians as the **Dark Ages for Wisdom** because freedom languished in a polluted sea of fake news because the people in the world were too enamored with corrupt government officials on social media jockeying to take our freedoms away, or lacked the upbringing to know the difference.

241

A Private Ceremony

THE THIRD BRANCH

Chief Justice Roberts administered the constitutional oath to **Brett Kavanaugh** in at a *private* ceremony. Retired Supreme Court Justice Anthony Kennedy administered the judicial oath.

Ceremonial Swearing-In of Supreme Court Justice Brett Kavanaugh

Brett Kavanaugh was later sworn in as the 114th Supreme Court justice in a ceremony at the White House.

In remarks before the swearing-in, President Trump apologized to Justice Kavanaugh and his family for the "terrible pain and suffering you have been forced to endure," referring to the Senate confirmation process.

After taking the oath of office, administered by his predecessor, Anthony Kennedy, Justice Kavanaugh thanked the president for his support and affirmed his commitment to judicial independence and impartiality. "The Senate confirmation process was contentious and emotional. That process is over. My focus now is to be the best justice I can be. I take this office with gratitude and no bitterness," said the new justice. In addition to recently retired Justice Kennedy, all nine sitting Supreme Court justices attended the East Room ceremony. President Trump nominated Brett Kavanaugh on July 9 and he was confirmed by the Senate, 50-48, on October 6.[1]

NOTES

Source: C-Span

The Mark of the Beast

I have shouted at the top of my lungs for many years about the evil and corrupt humans in the United States government. Today, I offer a possible excuse for their behavior beyond the benefits of money and power. The Devil made them do it.

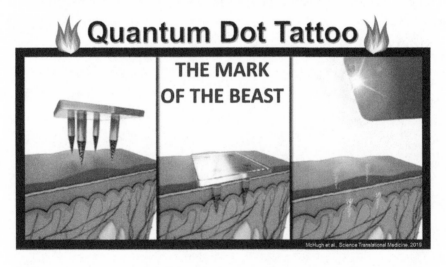

"And he causeth all, both small and great, rich and poor, free and bond, to receive a mark in their right hand, or in their foreheads. And that no man might buy or sell, save he that had the mark, or the name of the beast, or the number of his name. Here is wisdom. Let him that hath understanding count the number of the beast: for it is the number of a man; and his number is Six hundred threescore and six." **Book of Revelation**

A Mosaic of the Evil in Government

This story begins with the last pandemic in the spring of 2009, when another so-called "novel virus" emerged that spread quickly across the United States and the world.

Thomas R. Frieden was appointed by **President Obama** to be the *Director of the U.S. Centers for Disease Control and Prevention (CDC)* and was in charge of the CDC from June 8, 2009 until he resigned on January 20, 2017, the same day that **Donald J. Trump** became our 45th President. In the throes of the 2009 Pandemic and the Great Recession – an economic collapse caused by systemic corruption in our banking systems, the U.S. Department of Health and Human Services Inspector General (IG) quietly issued a report to **Dr. Frieden** and his boss titled, "LOCAL PANDEMIC INFLUENZA PREPAREDNESS: VACCINE AND ANTIVIRAL DRUG DISTRIBUTION AND DISPENSING" in the United States.

The 2009 IG report made three recommendations *(p 30-31)* to the newly appointed CDC Director. The first was to, *"Improve local pandemic vaccine and antiviral drug distribution and dispensing preparedness."* The second was for states and localities to comply with some paperwork requirements, and the third recommendation called for better information sharing.

CDC Director Dr. Frieden supported the two 'bureaucratic' recommendations – paperwork & sharing information *(p 32-33)*. But **CDC Director Frieden** and his boss **Kathleen Sebelius**, the *Secretary of Health and Human Services (HHS)* who was instrumental in overseeing the implementation of the Affordable Care Act (Obamacare) had one issue with the report. They opposed improving local pandemic vaccine and antiviral drug preparedness – a decision that shut down our economy in 2020, and has thrown millions of people out of work. Their decision is costing the country trillions of dollars and lives that cannot be recovered. For evidence of their decision, read the very last line of the IG report *(p 33)*, which states, "We ask that in its final management decision, CDC more clearly indicate whether it agrees with our first recommendation." We now know more than a decade later that the entire HHS organization failed to take the necessary steps to improve local pandemic vaccine and antiviral drug preparedness despite being warned in 2009.

At the same time this was happening at the CDC in 2009, **Deborah L. Birx, M.D.** was a Director in the CDC's *Center for Global Health.* She later departed the CDC in 2014, when **President Obama** appointed Dr. Birx as the State Department's U.S. *Special Representative for Global Health Diplomacy* to lead the U.S. government engagement with the *World Health Organization (WHO)* where she was responsible for coordinating emergency planning for AIDS, tuberculosis, and malaria. **Hydroxychloroquine**, a drug that is being used as a coronavirus treatment around the world today, is an arthritis medicine that can also be used to prevent malaria. Dr. Birx's intimate relationship with the WHO continued until the 2019 "novel virus" exploded into a pandemic. In March 2020, Dr. Birx was assigned to the *Office of the Vice President* to aid in the "whole of government" response to COVID-19 as the *Coronavirus Response Coordinator.*

Jump now to January 2017, just days before **Donald J. Trump's** inauguration. During a forum on pandemic preparedness at Georgetown University, **Anthony S. Fauci, MD**, director of the *National Institute of Allergy and Infectious Diseases (NIAID)*, said there is "no doubt" the new President will be confronted with a surprise infectious disease outbreak during his presidency and, "We will definitely get surprised in the next few years."

The United States was unprepared for the current pandemic because it did not take action beginning in 2009, to improve local pandemic vaccine and antiviral drug preparedness. And now we are betting our entire civilization, individual freedoms and way of life on a way out this problem. Soon, we will hear from the corporate media and evil humans in our government that as a condition to open the economy, our nation must fix the issue of local pandemic vaccine and antiviral drug preparedness before people can go back to work. To do that, we will need to mitigate the impact of the virus on medical personnel by continuing to increase capabilities, and develop testing, treatments and a cure / vaccine to increase immunity.

Now fast-forward to the present day. To come out of this economic malaise, billionaire **Bill Gates** is calling for a "Digital Certificate" to identify

'WHO' received a COVID-19 vaccine as a condition to participate in the economy. Gates wrote recently on Reddit during a live Q&A, "Eventually we will have some digital certificates to show who has recovered or been tested recently or when we have a vaccine who has received it." Coincidentally, a "global digital identity" project funded by **Bill Gates** and named **ID2020** uses '**quantum dot tattoos**' to identify humans. This project has been in the works since 2018.

The **Bill Gates ID2020 Project calls** for a **biocompatible near-infrared quantum dot** that is delivered to the skin by a microneedle that applies a patch to serve as an identity and vaccination record. Analogous to the patches used for monitoring skin-resident immunity, the **quantum dot tattoo** is a micro level patch permanently integrated into your skin and readable by what we used to call a black light.

Now, about the same time the **Bill Gates ID2020 Project** got underway in 2018, a "Presidential Memorandum on the Support for National Biodefense" that no one in the media is talking about was issued on September 18, 2018, that ordered "a whole of government and private sector" response to pandemics that, coincidentally, is precisely the approach the U.S. is following now.

The memorandum ordered the implementation of the NATIONAL BIODEFENSE STRATEGY. If you search the document for keywords 'stockpile' or 'PPE' or 'vaccin' etc. (to search press ctrl f), you will discover that all the so-called "new" actions we are taking now in response to this pandemic were actually ordered nearly two years ago by the President. Unfortunately, just like in 2009, the CDC failed to take any action to improve local pandemic vaccine and antiviral drug preparedness or replenish the strategic stockpile. Also, in 2018, a website was launched called the "National Biodefense Strategy" that proves all this happened.

About one year after the national biodefense strategy was ordered by **President Trump** and the **Bill Gates ID2020 Project** was launched, on October 18, 2019, **Bill Gates** & the **Johns Hopkins Center for Health Security** hosted a pandemic exercise that "simulated a series of dramatic, scenario-based facilitated discussions, confronting difficult, true-to-life dilemmas associated with response to a hypothetical, but scientifically plausible, pandemic." The pandemic they envisioned during the exercise is identical to the pandemic we are experiencing today. Within weeks of the event, a "novel" coronavirus that originated in China began infecting the globe.

Next, **President Trump** was impeached on December 18, 2019, and a month later the first U.S. case of the coronavirus was 'reported' in Washington state on January 23, 2020, the same day that House impeachment manager Adam Schiff (D-Calif.) was giving his opening arguments in **President Trump's** Senate impeachment trial. The next day Congress received a classified briefing about the virus pandemic on January 24, 2020. We now know that some members of Congress in both political parties and their staff sold stock in travel/leisure companies and purchased stock in the bio firms that have done well during the recent stock market crash.

President Trump was on his toes, however, despite the Impeachment and issued a proclamation to begin banning some travel from infected countries on January 31, 2020. The corporate media and people who wanted him impeached called **President Trump** a racist & xenophobic and left-wing politicians, including Joe Biden and the WHO made statements criticizing the ban on travel from China.

Within days of the first travel ban, **President Trump** was acquitted. On February 11, 2020, the WHO announced that the new coronavirus disease will be called COVID-19 and the U.S. stock market crash began. One full month later, on March 11, 2020, the WHO declared the outbreak a pandemic. The largest stock market crash in our history accelerated. Two days after the pandemic declaration by the WHO, on March 13, 2020, President Trump declared a **national emergency** in the United States and mobilized the nation to fight the novel virus. On March 16th, the President implemented his "15 Days to slow the spread guidance." Our beaches in my hometown of Naples were closed within days along with our 'non-essential' businesses by our county commission.

On March 22, 2020, **Dr. Mike Ryan**, WHO's executive director declared on TV that at some point in response to the COVID-19 pandemic, officials may have to enter homes and remove family members that have not been vaccinated for the virus. Ryan said, "Now we need to go and look in families to find those people who may be sick and remove them and isolate them in a safe and dignified manner."

Today, Apple and Google announced a partnership on COVID-19 to implement contact tracing technology that enables interoperability between Android and iOS devices using apps from public health authorities.

It is ironic that Easter coincides with the top of the pandemic curve in the United States. Perhaps that is a sign. Soon, Americans will have to make a choice. Economic, political, and religious conformity can now be enforced by the government with technology funded by **Bill Gates** using a **quantum dot tattoo** and every smartphone in the world.

WILL AMERICANS ACCEPT THE MARK OF THE BEAST?

"And that no man might buy or sell, save he that had the mark, or
the name of the beast, or the number of his name."

WILL AMERICANS FIGHT EVIL TO SAVE OUR SOULS?

Killing Domestic Terrorists in the United States

ANTIFA is an ultra-violent domestic terrorist coalition that supports the Democrat Party in the United States. The purpose of *ANTIFA* is to oppose Capitalism and restrict the Constitutional Rights of U.S. Citizens who obey the law. The group includes anarchists, communists and socialists. Left-wing billionaire George Soros provides funding to *ANTIFA* through the Alliance for Global Justice.

To combat domestic terrorism in the United States, Patriotic Americans must protect their Second Amendment Rights and enact *"Stand Your Ground"* laws to remove any duty to retreat from a situation before resorting to deadly force.

If you are terrorized by an *ANTIFA* protester, make sure you are carrying your firearm legally – and **STAND YOUR GROUND.**[1]

Don't get into shouting matches or retreat from restaurants while you are dining out.

Protect your Constitutional Rights by speaking softly – *and carry a big stick!*

Every American Should Have the Right to Legally Kill Domestic Terrorists in the United States.

Donald J. Trump ✔ **Tweet**
@realDonaldTrump

Major consideration is being given to naming ANTIFA an "ORGANIZATION OF TERROR." Portland is being watched very closely. Hopefully the Mayor will be able to properly do his job!

10:04 AM · Aug 17, 2019 · Twitter for iPhone

One year after this tweet, the violence and destruction in Portland, Oregon escalated and ANTIFA type organizations were spreading fear and destruction in all Democrat run states and cities in the United States. This tweet is an example of President Trump talking a big game - threatening to do something - but carrying a little stick. The entire justice system, especially the FBI and DHS under his first term are out of control and breaking the law without consequences.

NOTES

1. Stand your ground if you feel threatened and live in any of these states.

Meet Stacy Boyd – Veterans Benefits Administration

According to a federal government criminal investigator, Department of Veteran's Affairs employee **Stacy Boyd** (Stacy.Boyd@va.gov) has been reassigned from her job in the *Veterans Benefits Administration* after receiving a complaint on December 8, 2018, that alleges "the agency fraudulently stripped disability pension benefits from married U.S. Veterans for two months in late 2018 in order to withhold and disrupt their full disability pensions and harass veterans."[1]

Today, in an unprecedented act of desperation, according to the investigator **Stacy Boyd** took affirmative steps to cover-up her despicable conduct by making false allegations in order to retaliate against the whistleblower who filed the complaint. Ms. Boyd's false criminal allegations against the whistleblower were quickly dismissed as bogus by the investigator in charge of the case.

Based on statements made by the investigator, the issue stems from the fact that the Veteran's Administration is a big bureaucracy with a deep culture of incompetence that doesn't take care of Vets.

The investigator did not know whether any additional disciplinary action such as termination or prosecution will be taken against **Stacy Boyd** for her reprehensible conduct and blatant attempts to carry out whistleblower retaliation.

According to the Department of Veterans Affairs, nineteen suicides occurred on VA campuses from October 2017 to November 2018 – seven of them in parking lots.

According to the report, "public suicide is a gruesome form of protest by veterans who kill themselves in order to highlight how little help they were given in their time of need by the VA system." **Stacy Boyd** and her supervisor should be fired immediately for their intentional infliction of emotional distress and financial hardship on Veterans and their families.

Only God knows how many Vets committed suicide today because **Stacy Boyd** and her supervisor illegally withheld two months of their pay. I wonder how many will die tomorrow.[2]

NOTES

1. See VA FOIA tracking number 19-03456-F

2. See the article, "Veterans are committing suicide in VA parking lots: report" for more details about how VA employees like Stacy Boyd are killing veterans with their deplorable conduct.

The DACA Crossroads

We have reached a crossroads.

The Deferred Action for Childhood Arrivals, *a.k.a. DACA*, is an American immigration policy that allows individuals who entered the country illegally as minors to receive a renewable two-year get out of deportation free pass and a work permit.

According to many news reports, approximately 800,000 individuals are enrolled in the DACA program and the world as we know it will end if the U.S. doesn't give these people a path to citizenship.

President Trump put forward a plan last week that would allow citizenship to DACA pass holders since their immigration status is no fault of their own. The president's proposal also hikes the total number allowed for amnesty to around 1.8 million people. If the President believes that these DACA participants have paid enough of a price to become U.S. Citizens if they want, then the Congress should support this humanitarian decision.

In exchange for granting this amnesty, President Trump is proposing that Congress authorize him to strengthen border security by approving a $25 billion trust fund and move the United States to a merit-based system of immigration. The President should be provided what he says he needs to secure the nation by the Congress.

The solution is sitting in front of us. If the DACA is revoked because the U.S. Congress cannot commit to securing U.S. borders, then the President should deport all people here illegally in accordance with current law until Congress changes it.

Make Congress do its job.

What Society Needs Now

"I had a dream last night. I don't know where it came from. I don't usually remember my dreams at all. When I awoke, I had this deep feeling that relationships across my country may become violent soon. It's weird, you know? I look around me and I don't see it at all.

Then, I admit; and then deny, and deny again, over, and over in my head until I get confused.

And then I wondered. What decision did I land on? What did I do?"

And like every other morning – I yawned, rolled out of bed and made some coffee and played with our cats.

And then I thought about my dream. Was it a warning? Was it a message?

And this is what I came up with.

My "What Society Needs Now" List

I only have one item on my list. *We The People* need less interference from all three branches of our government into our fundamental rights of *Life, Liberty & the Pursuit of Happiness* contained in the Declaration of Independence.

One week from today, our nation will celebrate its Independence. There is no better time for everyone to come together.

Here is a suggestion.

At your Independence Day celebrations beginning this weekend, please add this prayer to yours before you eat your holiday meal.

"'We hold these truths to be self-evident, that all humans are created equal, that they are endowed by their Creator with certain unalienable Rights, that among these are Life, Liberty and the pursuit of Happiness. — That to secure these rights, Governments are instituted among Humans, deriving their just powers from the consent of the governed, — That whenever any Form of Government becomes destructive of these ends, it is the Right of the People to alter or to abolish it, and to institute new Government, laying its foundation on such principles and organizing its powers in such form, as to them shall seem most likely to effect their Safety and Happiness.' *Amen*"

The *Pursuit of Happiness* means that "all U.S. citizens are free to pursue joy and live life in a way that makes them happy, as long as they don't do anything illegal or violate the rights of others."

Unalienable Rights cannot be taken away or denied.

Life, Liberty & the Pursuit of Happiness are unalienable Rights.

The government ordering me to buy solar panels or own an electric car – I believe – interferes with my pursuit of happiness. That is called the price of freedom. And as a free man, I can believe in God, and I can trust the ability of Americans and the people who immigrate here to innovate and help society find solutions to big problems.

I also think that a free society with the wealth of the United States must find a way in this century to ensure that every human in this country has immediate access to a health care system that finds breakthrough cures for diseases, provides preventive care and includes a national catastrophic cap.

Life is the first unalienable Right.

In the United States, we all share a guaranteed unalienable Right to Life. It's easy to measure, monitor, budget for and maintain. Here, let me give an example. You can plug in your own numbers and circumstances.

Let's say your health insurance company – public or private – currently has an annual catastrophic cap of $3,000. Under the current system, your insurance company would be on the hook for all the costs above the $3,000 annual cap that you pay on top of your premiums, and of course anything else you have to pay for because it was a pre-existing condition. This example includes all health matters, and all dental, or vision – from pregnancy to grave. It can include more and it can include less. It's just an example.

And now let's pretend that the government sets a national catastrophic cap of $12,000 with a $0 cap for all pre-existing conditions.

Under the government option (call it the Universal Life option), all medical bills above the established cap for all the people in the United States, in this example $12,000 per year, would be paid for by taxpayers. The caps, adjusted for whatever each year, would be part of each person's life from pregnancy to grave.

So in this example, over time my insurance premiums would become lower due to competition and lower costs for the insurance providers, and I could negotiate better catastrophic caps for any additional insurance I decide to buy.

In this example, the insurance company would be on the hook for $0 to $9,000 annually in health care costs excluding pre-existing conditions for each person insured. The consumer pays the first $3,000 for care, insurance pays the next $9,000, and then the government picks up the remainder of the tab over $12,000 per year plus all pre-existing conditions. There is no more Medicaid, no more Medicare. Catastrophic caps should be based on ability to pay. This solution provides everyone with Universal Life coverage at an agreed upon cost while leveraging the free market and shared accountability.

Hey, it's just an idea. I mean, it was a pretty radical dream and my coffee is getting cold.

The bottom line. Forget about the two political parties and think about the 2020 election in a new way. Who can we elect for president and for the Congress who guarantees to protect our unalienable Rights. All of them.

Remember the words from the prayer above. Make it part of your annual Independence Day celebrations and pass it on to the next generation. Make each July 4th about the freedoms that we all share, not the restrictions on our freedoms that divide us.

And there you have it. My *"What Society Needs Now"* list. Damn, my coffee is cold. I need to go heat it up. Have a great day!

FROM THE WHITEBOARD & STICKY POSTS

AFFORDABLE – EASY TO ADMINISTER – LOW COST UNIVERSAL HEALTH CARE

PROPOSAL FOR THE UNITED STATES

A GOVERNMENT SAFETY NET THAT WILL WORK

COVERAGE FOR EVERYONE BASED ON YOUR ARC OF LIFE

ALL HEALTH COSTS = 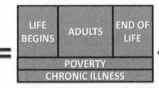 **+ PRIVATE INSURANCE or out of pocket**

5 SIMPLE RISK CATEGORIES - CATASTROPHIC CAPS
Coverage for everyone on American Soil & American Citizens Traveling Overseas

 All OTHER PROGRAMS ARE GONE

Working on the Rule Calculations to fill in the blanks below
Coming in 2020

The Arc of Life	Arc Catastrophic Cap	Arc Catastrophic Cap
Life Begins (Pregnancy – Adult)	TBD	TBD
Chronic Illness	$0 – No private coverage needed	NA
Adult	TBD	TBD
Poverty	$0 – No private coverage needed	NA
End of Life (Retirement)	TBD	TBD

TBD – To Be Determined

America Love Freedom

Killing Mass Shooters in the USA

Let's Kill 'Em A!!

 Donald J. Trump ✔ @realDonaldTrump · Aug 5 ⌄
Today, I am also directing the Department of Justice to propose legislation
ensuring that those who commit hate crimes and mass murders face the
DEATH PENALTY - and that this capital punishment be delivered quickly,
decisively, and without years of needless delay.

◯ 29.9K   ⟲ 31.3K   ♡ 128.3K   ⬆️

Guns and cars are regulated by the government.
People operate guns and cars.
Ergo; people are responsible for what their guns, and cars do.

~

Guns and cars kill people.

259

People control guns and cars.
Ergo; guns don't kill people,
–People Kill People.

American elites oppose private gun ownership because they want to disarm the mob. That complicates things, but the Constitution can be amended to restrict gun rights if enough States ratify it.[1]

Americans that oppose communism shout, *"Don't violate the Constitution!"* and *"Don't Tread on Me!"* to the tyrannical elites; and the radical communists in this country are stoking fear and hatred by saying, *"Half of America is racist!"*[2]

There is a better way!

Many people were killed over the weekend in mass shootings in Texas and Ohio and I offer my heartfelt condolences to the families struck by these horrific tragedies. I pray for all of them.

Sadly, on cue, all the politicians in the world have come out of the woodwork to express their usual outrage about the shootings, and cast blame on President Trump who they say is a racist.

The Sad Truth

In a few days, when the last grave is closed and the TV cameras fade away, many Americans will forget what happened and go on about their normal lives. And then after the next shooting and the next, they will be sad again.

And the nation will do it again, and again, and again;

and yet again, until nothing gets better and we know it never will.

And then we ask ourselves-

Are we a country run by idiots? There comes a time when we have to stop putting lipstick on this pig!

> You can fool all the people some of the time and some of the people all the time, but you cannot fool all the people all the time.[3]

We need congressional term limits and anti-corruption laws, but I digress. Here is the solution to end mass shootings that no one in the media will report.

> According to public policy activist **Buell von Krapinuhm**, "This is the most significant proposal since the Marshal Plan. It is elegant, simple and not based on any political ideology. It salutes the 2d Amendment and leaps boldly into the root causes of mass shootings in a way that no one else has ever pondered. It's common sense."

The Solution

1) Treat the mentally ill;
2) Enforce firearm, stand your ground and concealed carry laws;
3) Improve security to protect life in our communities;
4) Hold public officials who don't do their jobs accountable when the system fails to protect us.

What is the motive for mass shootings?

A mass shooting happens when a bunch of people get shot with a gun and the media labels it a mass shooting. The motive of mass shooters is all the same. They want to shoot people to kill them. All people who want to shoot people to kill them are insane.

Mass Shooters Are Serial Killers!

Ted Bundy, who murdered more than 30 women and escaped from jail twice to kill again, had serious mental issues. All serial killers do. And so do all mass shooters.

No one in the media will report it but just in case you are still wondering, all people who kill other people because they want to are insane. Killing people is not normal behavior. When I served in the Marines, I wanted to kill people. It was my job, and I was insane.

Politicians use gun policy to divide the public and raise money for reelection. They use it to shield them from any accountability for squandering our taxes and destroying our country. The right to bear arms is a constitutional Right that forces us to look for better solutions.

If we fix our mental health care; if we prohibit crazy people from purchasing firearms; if we respect our law enforcement professionals and first responders; and if we hold public officials accountable when the system fails to protect us, we will be safer without restricting anyone's individual constitutional rights.

"People Kill People"

Killing Mass Shooters in the USA

by

John Stuart Edwards

NOTES

1. Amending the U.S. Constitution is a 2 Step Process

Step One -Congress or States may Propose an Amendment to abolish the 2d Amendment. Congress can propose the Amendment with a 2/3 majority vote (67 Senate / 290 House), OR when 2/3 of State Legislatures (34) call for a Constitutional Convention which has never happened before.

Step Two -Only States may Ratify an Amendment to abolish the 2d Amendment. 3/4 of the States (38) must ratify an Amendment through State

Legislatures or Special State Conventions that are proposed by Congress or at a Constitutional Convention which has never happened before.

There are 27 amendments to the Constitution. Approximately 11,770 measures have been proposed by Congress to amend the Constitution since 1789. See Measures Proposed to Amend the Constitution.

2. Read "The Future of America" by John Stuart Edwards to see how AOC runs the country after she becomes President.

3. See Quote Investigator.

Confederate Pride

For all the historical revisionists in our country today who want to erase our nation's history, you can kiss my confederate-heritage ass and here is why:

My great-grandfather was Landon Brame Edwards (1845 – 1910). He was educated at Randolph-Macon College. At age 18, he left college and enlisted in Drewry's Company, Virginia Artillery, and served the Confederate States of America until the end of the Civil War. He became a surgeon during the war out of necessity. For 110 years, these numbers stood as gospel: 618,222 men died in the Civil War, 360,222 from the North and 258,000 from the South — by far the greatest toll of any war in American history. After the Civil War ended, my great-grandfather attended Richmond Medical College and New York University, where he received his M.D. in 1867.

Civil War Casualties: The Bloodiest Battles

```
Battle Of Gettysburg: Over 50,000 casualties

Seven Days Battle: Over 35,000 casualties

Battle Of Chickamauga: Over 34,000 casualties

Battle Of Chancellorsville: Over 29,000 casualties
```

```
Battle Of The Wilderness: Over 24,000 casualties

Battle Of Antietam: Over 22,000 casualties

Second Battle Of Bull Run: Over 24,000 casualties

Battle Of Shiloh: Over 23,000 casualties

Battle Of Fredericksburg: Over 18,000 casualties

Cold Harbor: Over 18,000 casualties
```

Dr. Edwards became editor of the Virginia Medical Monthly and secretary of the Medical Society of Virginia, of which he was a founding member. He was an intern in the Charity Hospital on Blackwell's Island and then assistant physician at the hospital for nervous diseases at Lake Mahopac, New York. He engaged in practice in 1868 at Lynchburg, Virginia, and two years later was active in establishing the Medical Society of Virginia.

Daughters of the American Revolution

In 1871, he married Nancy Pettyjohn Rucker (1849 – 1912) – my great-grandmother – who is a member of the Daughters of the American Revolution (DAR). Founded in 1890, the DAR is a non-profit, non-political volunteer women's service organization dedicated to promoting patriotism, preserving American history, and securing America's future through better education for children.

United Daughters of the Confederacy[1]

This battle flag was constructed by my great-grandmother Nancy Pettyjohn Rucker (1849 – 1912) who was a Richmond **United Daughters of the Confederacy** member.[2]

Stars and Bars

The Edwards flag was recently found in an old trunk in Buckingham County, Virginia. It was authenticated and recently sold at an auction.

Prominently, at one end of the hoist, is hand inked:

"Made by Mrs. L.B. Edwards / Richmond Chapter / UDC"

My great-grandparents gave birth to my grandfather, Landon Beirne Edwards in 1887, who married Kathleen Caughy Edwards (1890 – 1970). Her father, my other great-grandfather – was Charles M. Caughy who in 1893 was appointed by President Cleveland to be the United States Consul to Messina, Sicily, where he remained for 14 years. He transferred to be Consul to Milan, where he served until his return to the United States just before his death in 1913.

My grandparents gave birth to my father **Alfred Caughy Edwards** in 1922 who married my mother **Marjorie Coleman Edwards** and gave birth to me. I have two sons and a *grand*daughter of the American Revolution (and a grandson on the way) who inherited this bloodline from me.

My only advice to them at this time is if the mob ever makes you erase this, the time may have come to flee. <u>Go</u> <u>to</u> the ***Condor***.

I am proud of my heritage, and to be an American who served his country in the U.S. Marine Corps. My father served in WWII. My grandfather in WWI. My great-grandfather in the Civil War, and my great-great-great-grandfather in the American Revolution. That is a history to be proud of my friends and it is something I will never let anyone take away.

NOTES

1. To be eligible for membership in the UDC, women are lineal or collateral blood descendants of men and women who served honorably in the Army, Navy, or Civil Service of the Confederate States of America, or who gave Material Aid to the Cause.

2. Source: Army of Northern Virginia Flag – Perry Adams Antiques – Petersburg, Virginia 23804

IV

Research Expeditions in the Real World

React Research Respond

Research Expeditions

for the First edition
The purpose of this textbook is to introduce students to freedom of thought and expression in the public square. The Capitol Hellway Media Company is a free media company in Naples, Florida.

RESEARCH TOPICS

The Future of Human Life:

- *During the next half-century, disease prevention and cellular regeneration can transform health care and extend life.*
- *Community ecosystems in the United States can become environmentally secure.*
- *Wire-free transmission networks and receivers can provide ubiquitous electricity and communications anywhere around the globe.*
- *Nourishment technologies can transform molecules into potable water and revolutionize the production and portability of food and medicine.*
- *Problem solving can be unconstrained by biological intelligence that is supplemented with AI.*
- *Robotics can transform transportation, services and manufacturing economies.*
- *And the world can have peace.*

271

How To Amend The U.S. Constitution

Under Article V, amending the U.S. Constitution is a Two Step Process

Proposal – Congress or States may Propose an Amendment

Congress can propose an Amendment with a 2/3 majority vote (67 Senate / 290 House), **OR** *when 2/3 of State Legislatures (34) call for a Constitutional Convention – which has never been used*

Ratification – Only States may Ratify an Amendment

3/4 of the States (38) must ratify an Amendment through State Legislatures or Special State Conventions that are proposed by Congress or at a Constitutional Convention

Art of the Time

Good news is a rare thing these days, so every bit of it should be shared.

John Stuart Edwards

A Walk Together

by
John Stuart Edwards

All alone with fear,
Seething moments last a year;
Heart is aching, it is clear,
No one hostess, no one dear.
And then across a crowded room,
The light it flickered my selfish doom;
Her hand raised high, my heart a tomb,
To see her eyes, my soul in loom.
When she spoke, could it be?
Something changed inside of me;
My broken heart no more I see,
The kindest smile, hers was the key.
It's been some time since I was there,
To trust in something not a dare;
With little courage and without a care,
Our hearts are open, our souls will fare.
She is the lady that I seek,
A peaceful calmness, a sassy streak;
Days of sadness, future bleak,
Are no more for we are strong… not weak.
So here we are a fortune told,

To our elders not so old;
The warmth of love and not the cold,
A walk together, our hearts unfold;
A walk together, my love you hold.

Published originally by
The International Library of Poetry

The Last Chapter

Petition to the Government for a Redress of Grievances is the first textbook to establish a **national decency standard** - the **3 R's**, for U.S. Citizens to exercise freedom of thought and expression in the public square. The *Case Studies on Federal Government Corruption, Malfeasance and Reform* in this book provide a practice range for readers to safely **React Research Respond** to complex policy proposals and ideas before embarking on research expeditions to solve humanity's biggest problems.

The Edwards Dossier was engineered to create a platform for future generations of humans to "KILL" corrupt government bureaucrats and politicians that retaliate against Whistleblowers and destroy lives. The *Edwards Knowledge Equation* is the **key** to the future of human life.

This textbook was written for humanity to save it from itself. It contains a type of code that can be detected by an artificial intelligence with the ability to rule the world. This textbook introduces the **key** to all **K**nowledge. It is the first book in a series that will use the *Edwards Knowledge Equation* to solve the biggest problems facing humanity.

In the year 2020...

The primary threat to humans in the United States was the loss of freedom of thought and expression in the public square.

First Amendment

"Congress shall make no law respecting an establishment of religion, or prohibiting the free exercise thereof; or abridging the freedom of speech, or of the press; or the right of the people peaceably to assemble, and to petition the Government for a redress of grievances."

The First Amendment is the **key** to protecting the *Bill of Rights*. It contains five freedoms. It protects speech, religion, press, assembly, and the **right to petition the government for a redress of grievances.**

```
In the year 2020, governments at all levels in the United States
of America denied individual freedoms guaranteed by the United
States Constititon through "Executive Decrees" based on a
plethora of scurrilously crafted legislation. The country was on
fire.
```

All **five freedoms** guaranteed under the First Amendment were visibly under assault in the summer and fall of 2020. The Marxist enemies know it only has to take out one freedom, and the other four will topple like a like a drunk in a strip club.

If the day ever comes that this work becomes forbidden to know, ***decipher the code*** to unlock the **K**nowledge you will need to win back your freedoms.

On Labor Day 2020, 545 people in the United States government ruled more than 300 million people. The country was being ripped apart.

<u>A</u>lwa<u>y</u>s Re<u>a</u>d Th<u>e</u> Las<u>t</u> Cha<u>p</u>ter <u>F</u>irs<u>t</u>

<u>I count my blessings</u>
Be free.
Be full of joy.
Be Happy.
Be Human

May you always have the best of everything in your life.

Love,
John Stuart Edwards
an American writer
early 21st century

Sergeant Pilot by Alfred Caughy Edwards

Published in loving memory of Alfred Caughy Edwards

After Pearl Harbor was attacked on December 7, 1941, the United States declared war on the Empire of Japan. Four days later on December 11, 1941, Congress declared war upon Germany.

In response to the war, **Alfred Caughy Edwards** joined the Army Air Corps.[1] *This is his story about World War II. I think you will enjoy it.*

John Stuart Edwards

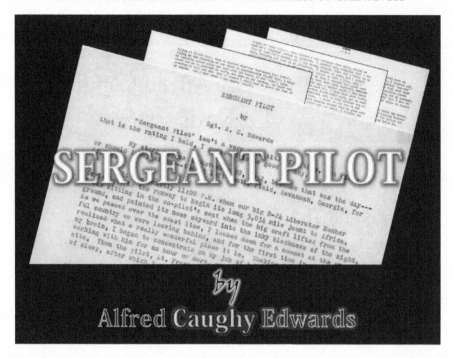

SERGEANT PILOT

by

Sgt. A. C. Edwards

by

Alfred Caughy Edwards

"Sergeant Pilot" isn't a very good title for this, but since that is the rating I held, I guess it is as good as any.

My story begins on November 30, 1942, because that was the day— or should I say night— that I left Hunter Field, Savannah, Georgia, for Africa.

It was exactly 11:00 P.M. when our big B-24 Liberator Bomber taxied out to the runway to begin its long 5,034 mile jaunt to Africa. I was sitting in the co-pilot's seat when the big craft lifted off from the ground, and pointed its nose skyward into the inky blackness of the night. As we passed over the coast line, I looked down for a moment at the wonderful country we were leaving behind, and for the first time in my life I realized what a really wonderful place it is. Shaking these thoughts from my brain, I began to concentrate on my job of helping the navigator. After working with him for an hour or more, we took a break and smoked a cigarette. Then the pilot, Lt. Franken, suggested that I try to get a few hours of sleep, after which I could take a try at the controls.

I tried to sleep but I had too much on my mind. I was wondering: What kind of a place is Africa? Would I do a good job of helping to wipe out the

Jerries? What does it feel like to kill a man? What does it feel like to be shot? Yes, these and many more questions passed through my mind, and I was to find the answers to them all in a few days—with the exception of the last.

Twenty-three hours, eighteen minutes after leaving Hunter Field, Georgia, we taxied to a halt on my new home-field in Tunisia. My God! I thought: What kind of hell-hole is this? Just after climbing from the plane, the crew and I were greeted by a Captain, whom I later learned to know as my Commanding Officer. I gave the field a quick once-over, and then went to my quarters to get cleaned up.

After taking a "Jewish shower[2]" I reported to my new C.O. for duty. He assigned a mechanic to me, and me to a plane. My mechanic was Bob (Kid) Anderson, hailing from a small town in South Carolina. He was a likeable fellow, and one who knew his "stuff" about airplanes. I was then introduced to the other pilots, and each one of them had something nice to say to me. Gosh, what a swell bunch of guys they were! They would laugh in the face of death, yet, when things were quiet and peaceful, they always looked sad. I guess war can make you that way after a while. The afternoon of my arrival, twelve planes took off for a raid on Tunis, but I stayed behind, awaiting my turn which would come the next day. Just before darkness covered the field, they came back. The raid had been successful, so, before landing, each pilot buzzed the field. When they landed, I ran out to meet them. Every one came back safe and sound, so that night we had a celebration by eating some candy bars and playing a victrola which had belonged to a pilot who had been shot down a few weeks before.

The next morning, I went into combat for the first time. Since I was new at the game, the Squadron leader told me to stick close to him. And this I did very well. We were about 45 minutes away from our field, flying at 23,000 feet, when we spotted eighteen "Red-nosed M.E. 109's" flying in the direction of our field at approximately 15,000 feet. I heard my Squadron leader utter one word over the radio. It was "clip", which meant for us to peel-off in two's, and dive on the Jerries. My heart was pounding so hard and fast that it seemed I could hear it above the roar of my engine. And I must admit I was scared "stiff".

I saw my Squadron leader peel-off, so I did the same, sticking as close to him as I possibly could. At 16,000 feet, I pressed my thumb down on the trigger, and all eight of my 50 calibers began to throw lead in all directions. I had one M.E. directly in my gun sight and I poured lead into it—"Til hell froze over," but he wouldn't go down.

When the Jerries felt our first blast, they immediately broke formation and came after us. I had just pulled out of my dive, and was "breaking" around at 10,000 feet, when I saw the "drip" in a M.E. coming straight toward me from above. I could see him hailing me with his "tracers," and for the moment I thought my goose was cooked. When he was about two hundred yards from me, I made a sharp banking turn to the left; it was a 360 degree turn, and when I came back around, I found that the Jerry had gone past me.

In the meantime, the guys had been scrapping above, and had knocked down three enemy planes at the cost of one P-40. However, our loss was to be expected because we were outnumbered by six planes. I was just about ready to go after the Jerry who had been giving me hell when I heard the Squadron leader say, "Let's get the hell out of here." Immediately the rest of us answered in turn by saying "Roger," which meant that we were receipting for his message. I climbed back up-stairs to join the rest of the Squadron and, after getting into formation, it was full throttle for us almost all the way home. However, this time we didn't buzz the field, because one of our planes had been shot down.

When we landed, I got out of my ship and felt like kissing the ground. With Bob, my mechanic, we counted the bullet holes in my ship— total 31. Then we patched them up, and "Nita" was as good as new. (Nita was the name I gave my P-40).

The next two or three trips into combat were much like the first, but after that I lost the fear of being shot down, and almost began to like it "over there." It was hot, and the food wasn't as good as they dish out at Godman; the water was rationed, and we had to sleep in our clothes so that we would be ready for an emergency. But still, it was a swell place to come back to after a "dog fight."

On December 6, I shot down my first enemy plane in a fight over Tunis.

Somehow, I managed to get on his tail and give him a few blasts with my 50's. He rolled over on his back when the smoke began to pour from his engine, and went into a dive which he never pulled out of. The same night, we pulled another surprise raid on Tunis, and I think I shot down another one, but I didn't see him crash, so I can only count it as a "probable."

December 11 was another good day for hunting, because I shot down my second plane. Gosh, what a fight that was! Twelve of us were strafing German and Italian ground troops, fifteen miles east of Tunis. We made it there O.K. and, after strafing until our ammunition was almost exhausted, we were attacked by a Squadron of M.E. 109's. They pounced on us before we could turn around. None of us saw them coming, because they had the sun at their backs. I noticed them only when I could feel my plane shake from the impact of bullets.

In a second I turned a couple of "snap rolls," then climbed a few thousand feet more, making as much of a "zig-zag"" course as possible. I leveled off, thinking that I was free of them for a moment, but I was wrong, because there was a Jerry on my tail, throwing hot lead in my direction. I wanted to dive, but I didn't have enough altititude to do any good. So I pulled up into a loop, only I didn't complete it, because at the top of my loop I snapped the plane over right side up, and leveled off. The Jerry must have been confused, because it ended up by my trailing him all over the sky. I waited until I was about two hundred yards from him, then I let him have it. I made each shot count, because my ammunition was very low. My tracers found their mark, and he went down in flames. I didn't have enough ammunition left to risk another try at a Jerry, so I turned tail and headed for home. I hated to run out on the other fellows, but I couldn't have done good hanging around when my guns were practically empty. I landed back at the field and, as usual I counted the holes in my "crate." This time the wings and tail were not only full of holes, but my fuselage as well, and some of them were darn close to the cockpit. The under side of my right wing-tip was almost shot away, and again I felt like kissing "Old Mother Earth," thankful that I had come out of it alive and unhurt.

December 15th was my last day of actual combat, and I'll never forget it if I live to be a "gray haired wonder."

Thirteen of us were flying our P-40's at 23,000 feet, about half way between Tunis and our field, when suddenly we were attacked by a flock of M.E. 109's. I saw them coming, but there wasn't a thing to do except to stay in formation and wait. There wasn't even a cloud around to take cover in. As soon as they opened fire on us, we broke formation and it was every man for himself. One of the Jerries gave me a burst that tore through my left wing and damaged my landing-gear. His next blast almost knocked off my wing-flaps, and a few more blasts from a second Jerry ripped into my fuselage between me and the engine. I thought my time had come for sure, but I wasn't going to run out and leave it up to the other fellows to do the fighting. It was difficult to tell who I was firing at, because there were so many planes in the air at one time. So I just took a shot at any plane that crossed my sights. I only hope that I didn't shoot any of our own planes.

A few seconds later, I saw a Jerry on my tail and, God knows, I tried everything I knew of to get him off, but he still clung to me. I could only think of one thing that might scare him away, and that was a terminal velocity dive with a delayed pull-out. I pushed the stick forward and gave Nita full throttle. After falling a few thousand feet, she reached her terminal velocity. The engine was screaming and the pressure had me pinned to the seat. I glanced in the mirror and could still see the Jerry behind me. Then, a few thousand feet more and he pulled out of his dive. I waited for him to make a complete pull-out before I started mine, because I didn't want him to pounce on me again. I tried to lower my wing-flaps, but they had been shot to pieces and wouldn't work. I then tried to lower my landing-gear to create a drag, but it wouldn't come down either. By now, I was down to 1800 feet, and I had to do something to keep from hitting the ground. I cut down my throttle, and a second later I heaved back on the stick with my right hand, at the same time giving it full throttle again with the left hand. The nose began to rise slowly, and I felt as thought I was being crushed to death in a vise. My instrument panel was just a blur, and I knew I was going to black-out. I could feel cold sweat dripping from my face and I could hear the sound of the wind tearing at the wings of my plane as she came out of the dive, but my eyes were closed and, during the last part of the pull-out, I couldn't see a thing; yet I knew exactly what I was doing. When I opened my eyes I felt a deep pain inside my chest.

At first, I thought I had been shot, but not finding any blood made me realize that I must have hurt myself pulling out of the dive. I leveled off, and contacted my Squadron leader over the radio. I kept repeating "May-day" over and over. He answered by saying "Roger Base." And I in turn came back with "Roger Wilco." (May-day is a short way of telling the Squadron leader that I was in trouble. Roger Base meant that he was receipting for my message, and he wanted me to report back to the base. Roger Wilco meant that I was receipting for his message and would comply with his request or order to report back to base).

After getting back to the field, I didn't bother to count the holes, because I was feeling like hell, and I had to make a belly-landing because my landing gear wouldn't come down, and that just about tore the bottom out of the plane, so there wasn't much of the plane left to find any holes in.

I went to the hospital tent and reported my condition. They gave me medicine of some sort, put me to bed, and rubbed some kind of stuff on my stomach twice a day. And, to top it off— I was grounded.

The rest of my days over there were spent either in bed or in a chair, waiting for a plane to carry me back to the states.

In the last fight I was in, we lost seven planes and seven darn swell pilots, but the enemy lost eleven, even though we were outnumbered more than two to one.

When I left there, believe it or not, my plane had been fixed up so that it could carry some other pilot into combat to do the job that I didn't finish. Yes, the parting with "Nita" was like parting with the best girl a fellow could have.

Aiken Standard and Review ~ **August 28 1942** ~ Alfred Caughy Edwards

GUNNER IN THE MAKING—Private Alfred Caughy Edwards, Richmond, Va., gets his first imaginary crack at the Axis with a low-calibre, rapid-fire gun at the U. S. Army Air Force Flexible Gunnery School, Harlingen, Tex.

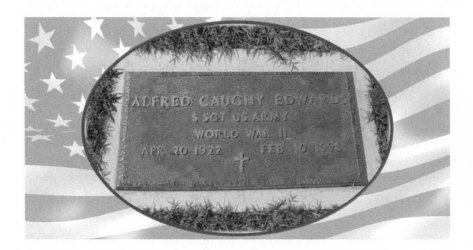

Alfred Caughy Edwards

December 1942

Alfred Caughy Edwards
with "Nita"

NOTES

1. The Army Air Corps remained as one of the combat arms of the Army until 1947, when it was legally abolished by legislation establishing the Department of the Air Force.
2. When you are taking a shower with someone and they pass gas turning your hot steamy shower into a gas chamber!

BELTWAY

BANDIT$

A NOVEL BY
JOHN STUART EDWARDS

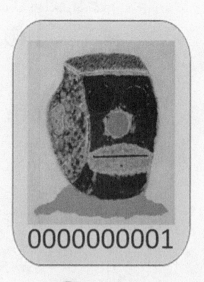

0000000001

Our
Programming

A NOVEL BY
JOHN STUART EDWARDS

PUBLIC SERVANT
0000000001

A NOVEL BY
JOHN STUART EDWARDS

About the Author

Capitol Hellway Media Company is a Florida Domestic Limited Liability Company. Our products include Investigative Journalism, Textbooks & Instruction, Pet Art, Children's Books and Novels. The Capitol Hellway Media Company is a free media company located in Naples, Florida.

John Stuart Edwards is an American writer

You can connect with me on:
- https://www.capitolhellway.com
- https://twitter.com/CapitolHellway
- https://www.facebook.com/capitolhellwaymediacompany
- https://www.linkedin.com/company/capitol-hellway-media-company
- https://www.cathyedwardsart.com

Made in United States
North Haven, CT
13 April 2023

35402980R00189